THE ARCTIC GUERRILLA

///DEFENDING ALASKA///

BY: L. SHANE LAND

shane.land@aw-sog.com

ISBN: 9798851039775
Imprint: Independently published
A Protected Work, 2023.

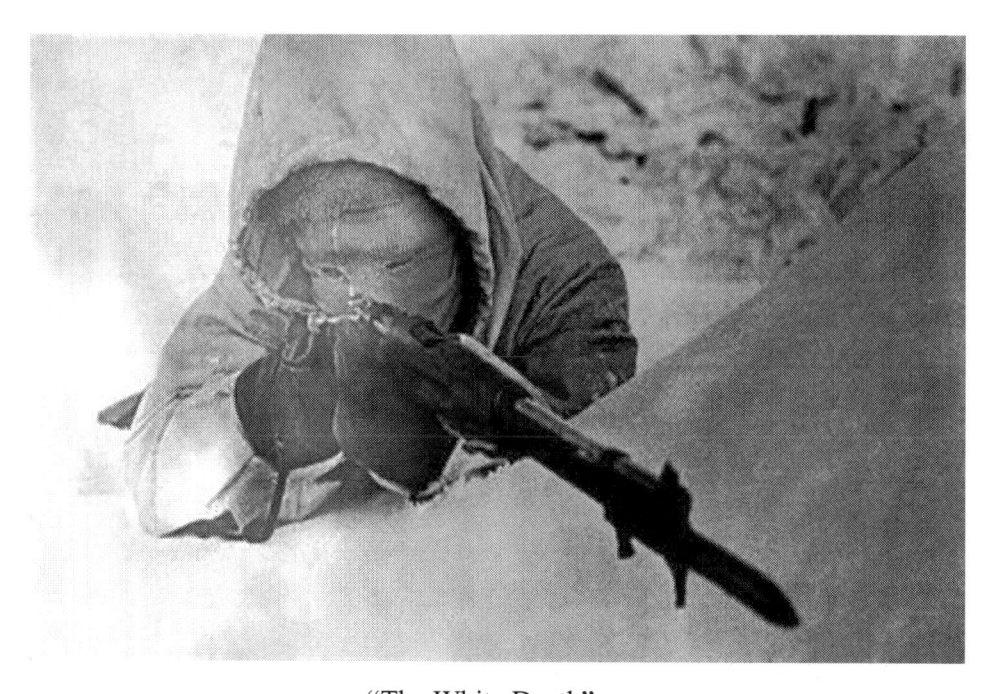

"The White Death"

Finnish sniper Simo Hayha during the Winter War in Finland. Retrieved from: https:// rarehistoricalphotos.com/simo-hayha-white-death-1940/

Table of Contents

In Memory of a Warrior	1
Dedication	2
Special Thanks	3
Disclaimer	4
Preface	5
Introduction	10

Part I

Ch. 1 Recognizing the Threat	16
Ch. 2 Initial Considerations	23
Ch. 3 Setting the Stage	26
Ch. 4 Ensuing Chaos	38
Ch. 5 The Asymmetric Arctic Environment	44
Ch. 6 Arctic Homeland Defense	51
Ch. 7 Challenges to the Defense of Alaska	57
Ch. 8 Train As We Fight	70

Part II

Ch. 9 Understanding the Human Terrain	79
Ch. 10 Relationships with Irregulars	84
Ch. 11 Culture	90
Ch. 12 Changing Perceptions	99
Ch. 13 The Alaska State Defense Force	106
Ch. 14 The Alaska Scouts	118
Ch. 15 The Arctic Guerrilla	122
Ch. 16 The Arctic Guerrilla Intelligence Network	136

Ch. 17 Arctic Guerrilla Medicine　　　　　　　145

Part III

Ch. 18 Amending Arctic Strategy　　　　　　153
Ch. 19 Conclusion　　　　　　　　　　　　　159

From the Author　　　　　　　　　　　　　　167
Acronym Glossary　　　　　　　　　　　　　　170
Resources and Reference　　　　　　　　　　　174

In Memory of a Warrior

Jeremy Wayne Linn
Captain, United States Army

3 November 1981 – 8 April 2014

Dedication

This book is dedicated to all the men of the 52nd Security Police Squadron's Combat Readiness Force (CRF) that I had the honor to serve with at Spangdahlem Air Base, Germany in the early to near mid-90's. For certain, we were the "Defenders" but in our own right we were also a band of guerrillas who received an unknown education in guerrilla warfare from one of the best team leaders anyone could ever hope to have.

Though I would begin my military career in the Air Force and finish in the Army, I have never forgotten the friendships I made at my first duty station. I salute each of you and *"Defensor Fortis"* my friends.

Mr. Bradley Young	Mr. Otis Hawes
Mr. Shannon Whtimore	Mr. Thomas Ewing
Mr. Derrick Austin	Mr. Jonathan Lopez
Mr. Ray Colhouer	Mr. Richard Smith
Mr. Jim Smith	Mr. Erik Blatnik
Mr. Joe Knapp	Mr. Barry Morris
Mr. Russ Thurman	Mr. John Fabbricatore
Mr. Jamey Harmon	Mr. Jarrod Richardson
Mr. Rich Leon	Mr. Jason Horst
Mr. Keith Wozniak	Mr. Marvin Gilley
Mr. Bruce Upperman	Mr. David Gallagher
Mr. Kenneth Patterson	Mr. Brad Pierce
Mr. Dennis McBride	Mr. Brian Smith

Special Thanks

I would like to say a special thank you to the following people:

Mr. T.R. Land	Dr. Dawar Sherzoy
Mr. Greg Kelly	Mr. Mike Jennings
Mr. Troy Perry	Mr. Mike Hoover
Mr. Wayne Hales	Mr. Fred Mead
Mr. Jerry Torres	Mr. Joel Pouliot
Mr. Robert Holbert	"Zeb" (you know who you are)
Mr. Matthias Sartorius	

Over a period of twenty plus years, countless hours have been spent engaged in highly educational discussions about several of the topics covered in this book and many that are not. From our conversations, all of you conveyed a remarkable amount of knowledge to me and I realized during the course of drafting this book that I have never taken a moment to say "thank you" for your gifts of knowledge as well as another "thank you" for your friendships. This is my way of saying "thank you" and to let each one of you know that even though we may not talk as much now as we did at one time, your friendships continue to mean a great deal to me.

I thank all of you for being such great friends, mentors, and advisors.

Disclaimer

All information presented in this book was obtained via unclassified, open-source means as well as from trusted and credible sources. To my knowledge, no information discussed or provided herein currently has any classification value. All information contained herein is public knowledge and easily obtainable through unclassified research. I neither had access to, nor did I read, any Classified version of any US Arctic Strategy published to date. Any information provided in this book which might be the same, or similar, to information provided in existing information found in any of the Classified Arctic Strategies is purely by chance.

This book has been self-published (a "sin," I know) and is based solely on my research, my analysis, my experience, and my thoughts. Various photographs retrieved from the public domain and from private sources have been inserted with locations and contributors cited. I maintain my own unique writing style so there are likely some errors in the pages that follow. I take full responsibility for all errors that may exist since I was the lone member of my editing team.

Preface

This book is primarily geared toward the Alaskan Arctic however, aspects of it can be applied near anywhere. With the exception of Chapter 3, which is a scenario created as a work of fiction based on historical actions, this book is composed entirely of factual information easily retrieved through unclassified, open-source research.

It was not until after the release of the "Resistance Operating Concept (ROC)" manual in 2020 that I began to shift my focus to examining how a war might be fought in Alaska should a foreign adversary invade. Little did I know at that time that in just under two short years, Russia would invade Ukraine and the Resistance Operating Concept would be implemented. What has taken place in Ukraine, if one reads the ROC manual, is a covert (albeit an overtly covert) proof of concept operation. This fact is easily discernable.

As I have continued to watch the war in Ukraine progress, it has been astounding to see the ROC "playbook" being utilized with such efficiency. How the population of Ukraine joined so quickly for the near "Total Defense" of their country and how external support from other nations ramped-up Ukrainian defense capabilities in such short-order is astounding. During this time, I began to ponder how the ROC would work on US soil if the need arose and only if everyone were at least semi-prepared to answer the call to Homeland Defense. It was with these considerations that I decided to examine the concept more closely while applying it to the current state of affairs in Alaska.

What resulted was my creation of the scenario that is discussed in Chapter 3 that was originally developed in the Fall of 2020. In late December of 2020 and early January 2021, I felt compelled to send the scenario to Commanding Generals of various military commands across the US. As expected, few responded.

The scenario developed rested squarely on three premises. They were:

> 1). If the Russians and/or Chinese were to invade Alaska, they would only do so in a remote geographical location that contained critical access to the most natural resources that they would be seeking.

2). The fact that remote areas of Alaska (in the far-removed areas outside of Fairbanks, Anchorage, and Juneau) must contain minimal to no military presence or immediate response capabilities.

3). The location would be a place which would provide the adversarial advantage of minimizing any resistance capability quickly due to a small population.

As a given "by-product" of the premises provided, an occupied area would become near immediately denied to friendly forces. This concludes that only the population would be in any position to oppose the occupiers by guerrilla or resistance means *if* they were adequately organized and prepared.

In this book, the words "resistance" and "guerrilla" are utilized interchangeably while fully comprehending that a resistance or guerrilla organization is comprised of more than just the stereotype of fighters who only engage in overt combat operations against the adversary. The utilization of the term "guerrilla" is done for no reason other than as a basis for describing the *type* of warfare conducted (call it unconventional or guerrilla or whatever may be preferred), not the political ideology or desired outcomes associated. The utilization of the term instead infers that resistance members do in fact include guerrilla warfare and/or guerrilla methodologies as a *means* to oppose occupying forces. While we have chosen to "soften" the adjective describing them, all are "guerrillas" at their core given that all utilize guerrilla tactics and methodology, whether covertly or overtly.

This is not a "How To" book on conducting unconventional warfare, resistance operations, or insurrection. This book is in no way any of these things should anyone attempt to argue to the contrary. Likewise, this is not a "prepper" book although some suggested preparation(s) will be discussed. There are countless historical books and videos on guerrilla/resistance tactics and techniques (as well as preparing appropriately) that are very applicable to the current situation being faced against near-peer adversaries, the climate, and the geographical terrain found in Alaska. What is identified in this book are two basic issues that tremendously hinder resistance/guerrilla operations and networks in the Arctic environment. The first issue is the fact that many remote locations (villages or communities) are typically small, containing small populations. As a result of the small nature of the village and its reflected population size, everyone will typically know everyone else, as well as everyone else's private affairs. The existence of such will prevent the Arctic Guerrilla from "swimming" freely amongst the population and/or, it will invite the unwanted attention of occupation forces directly to the village nearest to where activities are taking place. The second issue is that the harshly unforgiving climate of Alaska and other Arctic nations will aid in preventing active resistance operations, especially during the winter months. This implies that more passive resistance measures must be implemented during those times. These identified issues are more advantageous to the occupation forces than they are to the resistance or guerrilla organization.

While the issues discussed tremendously hinder the resistance, the movement is alternately provided with an advantage. Many members have detailed knowledge of a vast wilderness and terrain where they might maintain the ability to disappear, regroup, or base operations from. However, disappearance into the wilderness of Alaska (or any Arctic environment) and establishing a base of operations is only possible if those who do so are capable of *surviving and thriving* in the extremely unforgivable environment. While there are occasional villages scattered throughout the Arctic (and Alaska) landscape for potential rest and refit purposes, they are typically great distances apart. As well, simply going across the border to recoup until the next fighting season begins will probably not be an option such as it was for the Taliban and other resistance fighters in Afghanistan.

This book will examine identified deficiencies in current the US Arctic Strategy and discuss some potential alternative concepts for inclusion consideration. To say that all current US Arctic strategies are flawed would not be accurate and, in all honesty, would be rather unfair. Portions of each strategy written are comprehensively sound however, all miss critical points on specific subjects which they identify within their strategies. If the Department of Defense and each respective military branch would work together on a Joint Arctic Strategy, many of the subjects discussed in this book would likely be addressed and included into a new Joint Publication.

It is with hope that this book provides some insight for military leaders and policy makers as to what is currently absent from the Arctic Strategy.

However, it is very probable that many will continue to choose not to listen to what others outside of their professions are saying. If this is the case, then warriors will arise out of necessity, and they will do so without any prior support, planning, or preparations. These warriors will wear no formal uniform, and they will be more likely to identify ideologically with preservation of family, community, and self instead of that of any national ideology decided upon by policy makers in Washington. Members of the civilian population could very well be those primarily responsible for defending the US Homeland in the Last Frontier against adversarial incursion. The Arctic Guerrilla could be the first, and possibly the last, line of defense for the US homeland in America's Arctic if current strategy and mindsets do not change.

What is taking place in America's Arctic Region is that policy makers and strategists are, astoundingly, following a similar approach to a conflict in another region of the world some 60 years ago in a place where the climate, the terrain, and the enemy were all vastly different. That region and conflict was Vietnam and the approach and ending there was tragic. To effectively reinforce my sentiment, the words of former Kennedy Administration Secretary of Defense Mr. Robert McNamara are provided. In his book, *"In Retrospect: The Tragedy and Lessons of Vietnam,"* McNamara writes:

"I had never visited Indochina, nor did I understand or appreciate its history, language, culture, or values. The same must be said, to varying degrees, about President Kennedy, Secretary of State Dean Rusk, National Security Adviser McGeorge Bundy, military adviser Maxwell Taylor, and many others. When it came to Vietnam, we found ourselves setting policy for a region that was terra incognita."

McNamara's statement can be carried forward 60 years and now applied to America's Arctic as it is also a region that undoubtedly remains *"terra incognita"* for most US leaders and US forces, to include those stationed there. Anyone writing policy and strategy related to the Arctic Region from the confines of climate-controlled offices simply does not maintain any type of appreciation for the complexity of the Arctic and/or Alaska. This type of approach to the Arctic Region, and the type of warfare that will be conducted there, is completely out of touch with the reality of the situation on the ground. In openly stating this, the approach to the Arctic is very much presenting in the same manner as was experienced, and learned, in both Vietnam *and* Afghanistan.

Thus far, there has been nothing more than an abbreviated approach to the implementation of the US Arctic Strategy. I hope that the information provided in this book will change that. In order to effectively understand this environment, one must spend significant amounts of time exposed to it, live somewhere close to it, or seek out knowledge from those who are the true subject matter experts.

Introduction

This book has been written because the facts of this matter should be told and because all Alaskans, and all Americans, have a right to know exactly what is taking place regarding Homeland Defense in America's Arctic. This book does not address any other currently identified internal issues by the President, the Secretary of Defense, or the Chairman of the Joint Chiefs of Staff as being the greatest threats to our National Security. Issues such as critical race theory, gender differences and equality, the combating of racism and diversity, or white supremacy will not be entertained or discussed. These "woke" issues being identified as the "greatest threats" to our nation are bogging down our military and impacting the defense of our nation as can be easily substantiated by the fact that overall military recruiting numbers have plummeted. According to the Secretary of the Army Christine Wormuth, the Army alone missed their recruiting goals by approximately 25% in 2022. Who do they blame? Those who offer criticism of the "woke" military agenda. Enough said about this.

To be forewarned, Chapters of Part I of this book will be exceedingly difficult to believe. However, presentation of the factual information illuminates only a very minute portion of why homeland defenses are degraded in America's Arctic (Alaska). Degradation is due in part to poor planning, poor preparation, poor attitudes, poor leadership, and poor implementation of the Arctic Strategy which has been ongoing for at least the better part of four years. Unfortunately, this has become the "status quo" for many people responsible for not only the defense of our nation, but also for the safety and security of the people of Alaska.

Since 2017, I have been closely monitoring the situation in the Arctic Region with our near-peer adversaries (Russia and China) and how their actions are directly impacting Alaska. As the situation currently exists, the US homeland is extremely vulnerable to attack through the Arctic and that is to mean Alaska. It is absolutely no secret that US defense capabilities in Alaska are diminished and/or antiquated. By the Department of Defense's own admission, as published in unclassified US Arctic Strategy documents, US forces are not adequately prepared, trained, and equipped for extensive military operations in the Arctic environment. In other words, the vast majority of our military forces are currently "combat ineffective" for any sustained Arctic operations which is a severe deficiency that will take years to correct. This is the truth, and our leaders have acknowledged this truth in their own globally published strategies. This critical truth, and several others associated with the current US Arctic Strategy, will be highlighted in Part I of this book.

The US can only consider itself an Arctic nation because of Alaska therefore, defense must be provided for all of Alaska's resources including the people. Yet, due to the apathetic mindset of multiple administrations and military leadership regarding the Arctic Region, our adversaries have expanded their dominance, grown more aggressive, and continue to endanger Alaska's resources (the people). The Russians and Chinese have been continuously given a "gift" by the previous and current US administrations and they have been most appreciative. Even after many years of delay and neglect, the US Government, the Department of Defense (DOD), and subordinate US military services finally began producing Arctic strategies though all fall short in inclusion of indispensable key aspects.

Within the 2019 DOD Arctic Strategy, as pertaining to US National Security Interests in the Arctic, it is written that interests in the region include that of, "defending US sovereignty and the homeland." The defense of US sovereignty and the homeland has never been more important than it is now, specifically when it comes to Alaska. While US Homeland Defense applies to the whole of the homeland, sub-categorization of Homeland Defense specific to the Arctic area of the US <u>must</u> be recognized. As is currently the situation, the US homeland remains tremendously vulnerable through the Arctic avenue of approach due to issues previously mentioned. A vulnerability that remains even though the degree of Russian and Chinese threats were officially recognized by US government agencies years ago.

So, if conflict with the Russians and/or Chinese were to take place on US soil in Alaska tomorrow, how would the US choose to fight in the Arctic environment? Obviously, some warfare would be conducted in a primarily conventional, force-on-force manner as this is what is seemingly being planned for, as well as routinely exercised, in accordance with existing US Arctic strategies. But when the dust of conventional warfare settles beneath feet of snow and ice and low lying, dense cloud and winter storm cover, the conflict will resort to a more resistance or guerrilla-oriented means. Yet is any portion of the Alaska civilian population being prepared or trained for such an event? Has any proper planning and preparation of the civilian population taken place for what may come and what might be asked of them if it does? To my knowledge, only a fraction of a fraction of this has taken place.

Planning and preparing to oppose adversaries in the austere Arctic environment with the same, or similar, tactics that would be utilized in opposing them in the more permissible areas of Europe (such as we are witnessing in Ukraine) is illusory for a conflict in the Arctic. As outward appearances have it, there has been little to no consideration given that relationships with Indigenous people, and the utilization of resistance operations/guerrilla warfare in the Arctic environment, will provide for the best advantage in an Arctic conflict. Also apparently overlooked are the adversarial military forces who are already trained and equipped to fight in such an environment. This misconception is based on how Russian forces have been performing in Ukraine which is intentionally deceptive if you believe the media. Based on these facts, it only stands to logically conclude that Unconventional Warfare (UW) and Resistance Operations (RO) will be required in the Arctic given that US forces, as readily admitted in their own strategies, are not prepared[1] for extended operations in the Arctic environment. With all of this now said, careful consideration must be actively given for the inclusion of RO into the existing Arctic Strategy. This is an assertion that is once again supported by the open admission related to the lack of US force readiness and capability for Arctic operations. The most effective way for US forces to sustain extended operations in the Arctic environment is through the utilization of the population and their resistance efforts.

Resistance Operations must be considered as an integral part of the layered approach to total defense of the US homeland in the Arctic of Alaska. However, planners have consistently overlooked this concept. RO must maintain some significance in Arctic Homeland Defense (AHD) planning and

---

[1] Lack of readiness and capability of US forces in the Arctic is identified in US Arctic Strategy.

preparations and then combined with the modification of existing concepts associated with Internal Defense and Development (IDAD) as are found being applied in Foreign Internal Defense (FID) programs utilized abroad. According to Joint Publication (JP) 3-22, FID is defined as:

"...the participation by civilian agencies and military forces of a government or international organization in any of the programs or activities taken by a host nation (HN) government to free and protect its society from subversion, lawlessness, insurgency, violent extremism, terrorism, and other threats to its security. The United States Government (USG) applies FID programs or operations within a whole-of-government approach to enhance an HN internal defense and development (IDAD) program by specifically focusing on an anticipated, growing, or existing internal threat. A FID program would typically be supported by the Department of Defense through routine security cooperation activities as part of the geographic combatant commander's (GCC's) theater campaign plan."

In following the guidance of FID as set forth in the JP, it should be discerned that the application of FID can be modified and readily applied to aid with US Homeland Defense in Alaska against an "anticipated, growing, or existing external threat" such as Russia and/or China. Through modifications and application of FID and IDAD concepts, which should be inclusive of RO, AHD capability could easily be extended to include continued deterrence, defense, and/or resistance in the event of, and during, external threat activities or occupation.

This book provides an "outside the box" perspective of the importance of RO being an essential concept of Arctic Strategy. Personal perspective has developed from resources inclusive of historic external threat activities in or near Alaska, historical concepts of UW that have been applied in the 20th and 21st centuries, FID, IDAD, Counterinsurgency (COIN), Low Intensity Conflict (LIC), and Homeland Defense (HD). This book further provides the future "Arctic Advisor" with overlooked ideas directly associated with UW methodology that can be readily modified and applied specifically for the purpose of US Homeland Defense and RO in the American Arctic.

"Russian Arctic Paratrooper"

A Russian Airborne Soldier after completion of an Arctic jump from near 30,000 ft. Photo by Alexei Yereshko/TASS. Retrieved from: https:// www.dailymail.co.uk/news/article-8265519/Russian-paratroopers-wearing-oxygen-masks-white-camouflage-jump-33-000ft-Arctic.html

Part I

Chapter 1

Recognizing the Threat

For over two decades, the US has focused its diplomatic and military efforts into combating terrorism and quelling the insurgencies in Iraq and Afghanistan. In the midst of these operations abroad, the US has been inattentive to the fact that President Vladimir Putin and the Russian Federation have quietly strengthened their military and strategic presence in, and around, the Arctic Region. The strategic positioning of military capabilities now overtly and proudly possessed by Russia has gone mostly unaddressed by four administrations[2] of the US since 2001. The question arises, has the US failed *to acknowledge and to respond* to what can only be described as the ever-increasing Russian dominance of the Arctic Region? This chapter will answer the question.

There must exist recognition and acknowledgement of the threat and the threat potential to US Homeland Defense through Alaska pertaining directly to a Russian and/or Chinese invasion or occupation in order to acquire at least a portion of the territory. It stands as fact that recognition of the threat has already been publicly made by the DOD and the Director of National Intelligence (DNI). Recognition of the Russian and/or Chinese threat, by both offices, has been justly identified as primary and is of significant importance in that it has been also duly recognized by National and US military Arctic strategies. In this regard, it would make sense that adequate preparations are being made accordingly.[3] As an integral part of preparation, steps towards AHD and resistance planning, development, and implementation *should be* well under way.

Critical perspectives which will assist in attempting to address the reasoning identified above are: 1). Identification and acknowledgment of the Russian presence in the Arctic through strategy, 2). Military recognition of the

---

[2] Presidents Bush, Obama, Trump, and now Biden have neglected the Arctic Region and failed to recognize its strategic importance.
[3] Recognizing the "2+3" aspect of the 2018 National Defense Strategy. Russia and China, then North Korea, Iran, and Violent Extremism (2+3). The Alaska Emergency Operations plan should be revamped to align with the current threat as presented in National Strategies.

scope of the Russian threat, and 3). Political recognition of the threat. All three perspectives align with the National Defense Strategy associated with the Arctic Region and all are addressed in the subsections that follow.

1. The first critical perspective is the appropriate recognition and acknowledgement of the issue related to the ever-increasing Russian presence and growth in the Arctic Region. The issue is clearly addressed within the DOD Arctic Strategy report to Congress in June 2019 as it states:

"Russia views itself as a great polar power and is the largest Arctic nation by landmass, population, and military presence above the Arctic Circle. Russia's commercial investments in the Arctic Region have been matched by the continued defense investments and activities that strengthen both its territorial defense and its ability to control the NSR (Northern Sea Route). Russia formed the Northern Fleet Joint Strategic Command in December 2014 to coordinate its renewed emphasis on the Arctic. Since then, Russia has gradually strengthened its presence by creating new Arctic units, refurbishing old airfields and infrastructure in the Arctic, and establishing new military bases along its Arctic coastline."

In consideration of the previous excerpt from the DOD Arctic Strategy, it is evident that the Department has not only definitively recognized the threat posed by the expanding Russian presence in the Arctic Region, but the Department has also acknowledged that the threat existed and has continued to grow significantly since at least December 2014. Yet even though the significance of the Russian threat in the Arctic Region has been presented in the DOD document, the strategy itself presents as being nothing more than a "paper tiger." Whilst the strategy has continued to draw mostly infrequent attention and collects dust on a shelf, the Russian's have remained active in their relentless pursuit of Arctic Region domination.

2. The second perspective was openly expressed on two previous occasions by the former Commanding Officer of NORAD and USNORTHCOM, General Terrence J. O'Shaughnessy. In remarks made to the US Senate Armed Services Committee in February 2020,

General O'Shaughnessy expressed his concerns about the expanding Russian presence in the region in conjunction with upgraded long-range bomber capability and new warships capable of cruise missile transport and/or a payload delivery in American Arctic Region (Berthiaume/Canadian Press, 2020). The General's 2020 sentiments echoed those he previously made in July 2019 before an audience at the Center for Strategic and International Studies in Washington. In a US Department of Defense news release related to July 2019, General O'Shaughnessy is quoted as saying, "But surprisingly, there is not that much conversation about cruise missiles. When I look at the cruise missile threat, I see that as one of the biggest threats we face (Lopez/US Fed News, 2019)." The remarks provided on both occasions by General O'Shaughnessy were delivered after the release of the DOD Arctic Strategy in June 2019. The stated, and then echoed, remarks provide critical insight related specifically to the magnitude of the Russian threat in the Arctic Region as identified by the then top-ranking military officer of two Commands. However, the hesitation to implement the Arctic Strategy has remained which only serves to pave the way for the Russians, and potentially the Chinese, in the region.

3. The third and final perspective arrived by means of political agenda in Washington, D.C. in late October 2019 on the floor of the United States Senate. Alaskan Senators Lisa Murkowski and Dan Sullivan presented a Bill to the Senate calling for the creation of the Department of Defense Arctic Security Studies Center (Sjordal/KTVF, 2019) in Alaska. In an excerpt from her speech to colleagues in the Senate, Senator Murkowski stated the following:

"We see Arctic security emerging as an area of threat as well as interest as it certainly remains the likely spill over conflict area should confrontations occur within Europe or Asia. So great scholarships plus international and interdisciplinary engagement from an Arctic center would help advance defense readiness, develop Arctic awareness, and improve allies and partner capabilities to support multinational security cooperation across the circumpolar Arctic (Murkowski/Press Release, 2019)."

As related to Senator Murkowski's statement, there is revealed a sense of urgency by at least some politicians regarding the issues of both National Defense and International Relations which directly apply to the Arctic Region and *all* Arctic Nations. While the proposal was finally passed by Congress in December 2020 and the center officially stood-up in June 2022, the US has continued in a direction which is slow to implement Arctic Strategy and thereby appears purely reactive (mostly inactive) to Russian and Chinese progress in the region. This only aids in acting as an enabler to adversarial initiative.

There also exists some contributing factors which have led to Russian dominance in the Arctic. This is inclusive of America's strategic focus in other regions, outright neglect or dismissal of the Arctic issue, and the lack of implementation or adherence to existing strategy. Compounding these factors is the prospect that US planners and policy makers simply do not comprehend Putin's strategic planning or even the man himself. Working in tandem, all of these factors have created what can only be described as a "New Cold War" (Schoen/Smith, 2016) which has emerged on the fringes of the far northern frontier of our homeland.

Since 2001, US policy makers, administration officials, and military leaders have actively focused strategy elsewhere (Fry/Military Review, 2014) due to ongoing deployments of personnel, the conduction of operations, and numerous policy shifts related to counterterrorism and COIN. Speculatively, global focus by US and NATO in other regions have provided the Russians with a window of opportunity to focus their efforts on the Arctic. Stated conceptually, the Russians capitalized on America's distractions and geographical absence and utilized these to their strategic advantage which permitted growth and dominance in the region. In doing so, the Russian's have far surpassed the US in the Arctic while also significantly reducing US progress there. As related to global powers in a game of chess, the Russian move has resulted in "check" to the US. Russia's move must now be countered in a purely reactive response by the US and the question which the US must face is if the move is "too little, too late?"

In the article, *"Russia Expands Military Presence in the Arctic,"* which appeared in *National Defense* in December 2015, Ms. Sharon Burke, a senior advisor at the New America Foundation's International Security Program was interviewed. Ms. Burke expressed that the US must take what Russia is doing in the Arctic with a "grain of salt." She further states:

"Russian statements about their resurgence and about their military intentions, we have to take very seriously. They are a serious country with a large military and advanced defense infrastructure. However, just because President Putin says 'jump' doesn't mean we should jump. The Arctic remains a very challenging environment, a very difficult place to have troops and equipment stationed, and that's going to be true for a very long time (Tadjdeh, 2015)."

Ms. Burke's statement came just months after the Russian's conducted an Arctic military exercise comprised of "eighty thousand troops, 220 aircraft, forty-one ships, and fifteen submarines (Schoen/Smith, 2016)." In the consideration of Ms. Burke's statement, in conjunction with the status of Russian dominance now presented in the Arctic Region as of the end of 2022, one must wonder if others also feel compelled to take what the Russians have done in the Arctic "with a grain of salt."

While defense officials and some politicians have actively monitored and reported on the increasing Russian presence in the Arctic, it is mostly apparent that none of the reports are being seriously considered by many in Washington. An example is that of the previously mentioned Bill introduced to the US Senate by Alaskan Senators Lisa Murkowski and Dan Sullivan (Sjordal/KTVF, 2019) calling for creation of an Arctic Region Security Studies Center. As discussed, the Bill sat idle until finally being passed in December 2020. In addition, the continued US neglect of the region, even after the regional importance of the threat was identified in the NDS and DOD Arctic strategies, has provided President Putin and the Russian Federation (and potentially the Chinese Communist Party and Xi as well) with a continued reward of the initiative. Providing the Russians (and Chinese) with any initiative in the Arctic Region becomes even more dangerous and alarming when considering the close geographical physical proximity of their forces and capabilities in relationship to both the US (Alaska) and Canada.

The threat to Arctic Homeland Defense is very real and openly exhibited by the frequency with which Russian aircraft are intercepted by US and Canadian fighters off the coast of Alaska. From 2018 until as recent as the present date, numerous Russian aircraft (inclusive of reconnaissance planes, long-range bombers, and fighters) have been intercepted off the Alaskan coast. This statement was previously reinforced in an *Air Force Times* article on 28 April 2021 by Alaskan Command Commander LTG David Krumm. LTG Krumm stated that, "We intercepted over 60 aircraft last year...We monitored more than that." There was even an interview conducted by Brian Kilmeade of Fox News with former NORAD/NORTHCOM commanding General O'Shaughnessy on 9 April 2020 (Kilmeade/Fox News, 2020) which discussed a 2020 event that had taken place earlier that year.

In providing an additional assessment, a frequently overlooked part of the equation is the potential for strategic brilliance related to Arctic expansion exhibited by Vladimir Putin. One really must search no further for an example of his strategic achievement in the Arctic than the illustrated accomplishment of his goals there that have been all but absent of any US or NATO infringement. Putin's accomplishments of these goals and how he achieved them should not be so easily dismissed as purely coincidental, "dumb luck," or taken with a grain of salt. Though the Russians are currently involved in conflict with Ukraine and some civil discord transpiring withing the Russian Federation itself, Putin prevented the Russian Federation from being drawn into the quagmires of both Iraq and Afghanistan which are locations that he watched plague his adversaries in NATO for two decades.

Where Putin did commit forces, in places such as the Balkan States or even briefly in Syria, he did not commit them for any extended duration (Schoen/Smith, 2016). Putin's decision not to over-commit his forces in these regions tremendously aided him in further pursuing and attaining his goals in the Arctic. Putin also capitalized on the unexpected Syrian refugee crisis, exacerbated by the brief Russian intervention in Syria, which placed tremendous strains on several State economies. This pleasantly unexpected exacerbation also assisted him in utilizing additional distractions to accomplish his goals elsewhere. In again referencing chess, Putin read the board and never lost focus. He strategically positioned his pieces and dictated that his adversary must respond reactively and defensively in order to "set the board." In likening the chess game to the Arctic Region, Putin has controlled "the board" for nearly two decades.

The question posed at the outset of this section was, "Has the US failed to appropriately acknowledge and respond to the increasing Russian dominance in the Arctic Region?" It is believed that this question has been answered by the argument presented in this chapter as discussed within the critical perspectives. The US *has failed* to appropriately acknowledge and respond to the increasing Russian dominance, and threat, in the Arctic Region. It appears that the US strategy related to the Arctic Region has taken on a "hurry up and wait" mentality for at least a decade and this approach has now proven costly. When logically considered, the overall lack of US Arctic Strategy implementation has provided the Russian Federation with tremendous latitude in achieving their goals in the Arctic Region as they remain almost completely unopposed. The fact that the US has neglected or dismissed Russian Arctic dominance has now created the potential for catastrophic consequences to the US homeland through Alaska.

Chapter 2

Initial Considerations

In believing that conventional warfare in the Alaskan Arctic would quickly run its course thereby causing a shift in the conflict to more unconventional means, the scenario developed in 2020 and discussed in the following Chapter is based on what is deemed to be the most immediate strategic location that our adversaries would want to invade and/or occupy Alaska in order to gain a "foothold" on US soil. The scenario is by no means all-encompassing however, it has been determined to be plausible in order to place the reader into a "guerrilla state of mind" moving forward. Prior to presenting the scenario, some additional information should be offered.

Based on analysis, it is unlikely that a Russian or Chinese (or Russian-Chinese combined) invasion of Alaska would include the *whole* of Alaska. Attempting an invasion of this magnitude is neither logical nor relatable to short or mid-term Russian or Chinese interests or goals in the Arctic Region. It has also been witnessed in Ukraine that the Russians do not maintain the assets, the logistical capability, or support (at this time) for such an ambitious endeavor. They should have instead focused their efforts on small scale operations in Eastern Ukraine in order to seize and hold the territory. Lesson learned for the Russians. No doubt China, as well and North Korea, has been paying particular attention to Russian operations and NATO's response in Ukraine and would likely utilize their knowledge of lessons learned from both sides for advantages in an Arctic conflict.

It is far more logical to believe that key strategic locations such as military facilities and critical infrastructure in Alaska would be targeted by foreign forces instead of a full-scale invasion of the State. This belief rests in conjunction with key terrain and weather being utilized to their strategic, operational, and tactical advantages. Elimination of selectively targeted US strategic locations deep within Alaska and along coastal areas would assist in obtaining an outlying "foothold" for enemy forces with their primary objective being that of further occupation of vital areas that contain, or have access to, many of Alaska's valuable natural resources.

In corresponding with the assessment made in the previous paragraph, it should also be considered that external threat forces would likely utilize the extended winter season of Alaska *for offensive operations* in order to expand their area of occupation and influence to align with Spring and Summer objectives. Conduction of winter operations would present with little opposition as is evident in US Arctic strategies. This consideration is one that is believed to be mostly unanticipated by US military planners as related to adversarial Arctic operations during winter months.

The justification for the previous assertion is based on the fact that for several years now, both Russian and Chinese military forces have been actively equipping, training, and preparing extensively for warfare in harsh Arctic conditions. Why maintain dedicated Arctic units if they do not maintain this capability and if not for this specific purpose? Further substantiating this assertion is the fact that winter operations have been utilized by Northern European countries for centuries in conduction of offensive operations with the best time for these operations being identified as mid-winter to early spring, prior to break-up (Tuunainen, 2014).

In all probability, both the Russians and Chinese have accurately assessed that US forces in the Arctic are ill-prepared for extended combat operations in severe cold-weather conditions, even in Alaska. Presumption of their assessment can be validated by the open admission of the lack of US preparedness and effectiveness as described in published US strategies. Currently, US defense of the homeland through an Arctic avenue of approach is minimal. This fact warrants a critical evaluation of US Arctic Homeland Defense in order to accurately, and honestly, ascertain where capabilities are inadequate or, moreover, they are non-existent.

In the event of adversarial first-strike operations conducted against Alaska, it should not be expected that US military assets and personnel already positioned there are capable of sustaining operations for an extended period or even until re-enforcements arrive in accordance with any Order of Battle. It would be strategically advantageous to our adversaries if, in a first-strike operation, they destroyed not only our ability to project our own forces internally, but also destroyed or tremendously diminished our capability of *receiving* external friendly forces simultaneously. An honest assessment of the current AHD situation should be inclusive of critical factors relating to a "Red

Team" assessment of the adversarial understanding of the operational environment as *they* know it. This assessment should honestly and accurately measure current US defense capability in strategic locations of Alaska as compared to Arctic adversarial capability and probable intent.

It has been determined that one of the most favorable locations for an initial adversarial incursion into Alaska would be Nome. Nome maintains little by way of a military presence, or even a defensive capability, other than law enforcement personnel and armed citizens even though the location maintains both an active airfield and port. Nome is best suited for our adversaries and their immediate needs (objectives) to gain a foothold in Alaska and develop a capability to both receive and project occupation forces forward from the location.

In consideration of this analysis, what do US forces in Alaska really know of Nome? Has there been a site-survey conducted in order to determine strengths and vulnerabilities? Are both the formal and informal leaders of Nome and surrounding areas known to US leaders and planners? What do they know of the population and Native cultures there? Have there been assessments made related to the population's sentiment towards governance? Has an assessment been made as to how the population could assist US efforts if the area suddenly became denied? Has there been an assessment of critical infrastructure (such as airfield, port, medical, water supply and purification ability, electrical supply, etc.) compared with known adversary asset capabilities of forward operational units? Has an assessment been conducted as to how terrain and historical weather trends of Nome could be utilized by our adversaries to their advantage? Questions such as these could go on and on and all are critical information requirements which should be known, not speculated.

A location such as Nome would be strategically important to our adversaries due to the intact critical infrastructure necessary to support insertion of follow-on forces and projection of those forces throughout Alaska. Given the strategic importance of an area such as Nome, the scenario in the following Chapter was created to demonstrate the relative ease with which Russian and Chinese forces could invade the US homeland in that specific location.

Chapter 3

Setting the Stage

As stated, the following scenario was created in the Fall of 2020 with it being sent to Commanding Generals across the US in late December 2020 and early January 2021. As also stated, very few of them responded. Before you think that I might have been a bit "off my rocker" when I wrote this scenario, an interesting event happened in 2022 that gave tremendous credence to what I had previously written in 2020.

In 2022, an unclassified presentation/briefing was given in Alaska by two military visitors from the Naval War College which included a scenario involving a near-peer adversary's invasion of Alaska. An acquaintance who attended the briefing told me that what was presented was probably 90%, or more, "spot on" as related to the scenario that I had written in 2020. I do not know if my scenario had been passed on to others, but the fact that my scenario was so closely reflective of theirs (mine having been written some 15 months or so *before* their presentation) served to reassure me that I was on the right track long before they were. It was also very reassuring to know that I was not "off my rocker" in any way.

Alaska is an exceptionally large state and any attempt to invade the state entirely would be a failed strategic objective from the outset. It is suspected that only a region related to a sizable portion of Alaska's natural resources (oil, natural gas, etc.) would be a viable option for foreign adversaries. However, in order for foreign forces to obtain a foothold in the desired location, there must first be significant degradation, or even nullification, of US defense response and capabilities contained within Alaska itself. This goal could be achieved in many ways but for the sake of this scenario, it will begin with an effective naval blockade of the Bering Strait in conjunction with the strategic targeting of three internally located geographical areas by high-altitude detonation of tactical thermonuclear electro-magnetic pulse (EMP) weapons.

With the amount of increased activity of Chinese "weather balloons" and other as yet to be identified objects making their way through North American skies, it could be just a matter of time before one of these "balloons" is carrying a payload that could simultaneously darken considerable portions of the contiguous United States or Alaska. What is even worse to imagine is that one, or several, of the payloads attached could potentially contain biological weapons as well. Neither of these considerations are "far reaching" and in fact, should provide the North American population, specifically the population of Alaska, tremendous concern.

The following scenario was developed in order to "set the stage" for what an invasion of Alaska could resemble. It is by no means all-inclusive of events which could take place, however, it is a starting point for deliberation for both the population of Alaska and military forces already positioned there. As previously stated, the majority of this scenario was written in 2020, and remains applicable, while some updated material has been added in accordance with recent events.

Phase I

In the initial portion of Phase I, an invasion of Alaska by external threat military forces would begin without the majority of the population knowing what had transpired. An unassuming naval blockade of the northern and southern areas of the Bering Strait by combined Russian and Chinese naval forces could effectively create a corridor for invasion forces prepositioned in the Strait and in the eastern Russian Arctic. Under the deception of military exercises in the region, a combined effort by both Russian and Chinese air and naval forces could easily enter the area and establish a corridor across the Strait for follow-on offensive actions.

With the created corridor crossing the Bering Strait, Russian and/or Chinese container ships or submarines could execute precise targeting of pre-designated Alaska locations in order to darken a substantial percentage of the State and US defense capability there. Numerous US intelligence agencies report that Russia, China, North Korea, and Iran all maintain the capability to conduct such first-strike operations with the 3M-54 Kalibr missile, also known as the "Club-K." This missile can be armed with a High Explosive or Thermonuclear warhead, has a maximum range of 4,500 kilometers (km), with launch capability platforms being from a container ship or submarine.

Another strategic advantage provided by the Club-K is its low altitude flight capability (50-150 meters above ground level) which, in all likelihood, would remain undetected by US Early Warning Detection (EWD) sites in Alaska or elsewhere. If the Club-K were detected shortly after launch, it has a reported maximum flight speed of MACH 2.5-2.9 which is equal to 1,918-2,225 mph.[4] With flight speeds in this range, US missile defense in Alaska would have very little time to react for either response or intercept[5] especially if climbing to the altitude needed for detonation. In addition to the Club-K, there now exists the Russian "ready for war" missile known as the Avangard. The Avangard is a hypersonic glide vehicle capable of delivery of nuclear payloads for which the US currently has no known defense.[6]

According to an article by Mac Slavo, an EMP detonation approximately 300 miles above Nebraska would have the capability to render the entire United States, from coast to coast, helpless (see following illustration). With a "black-out" taking place across the US due to an EMP detonation caused by our adversaries, conditions would deteriorate quickly in major cities. With tensions already at "fever-pitch" across the US for numerous reasons later discussed, it would not take an extended period of time before many places fell into complete lawlessness and chaos.

From container ship or submarine launched platforms in the Bering Strait, 3M-54 Kalibr or hypersonic missiles could easily reach their strategically designated target destinations within, and over, Alaska in minutes. Doing so would render US defense capabilities either significantly degraded or completely nullified. Examples of strategically designated targeted locations could potentially be, but are not limited to:

1. Anchorage (briefly discussed)
2. Nenana (briefly discussed)
3. Kodiak (briefly discussed)
4. North of Fairbanks

---

[4] More information on the 3M-54 Kalibr can be found at the *Wikipedia* page https://en.wikipedia.org/wiki/3M-54_Kalibr
[5] Former NORAD/NORTHCOM Commanding General Terrence O'Shaughnessy voiced his concern over the cruise missile threat in 2019.
[6] CNBC article by Amanda Macias, 27 December 2019.

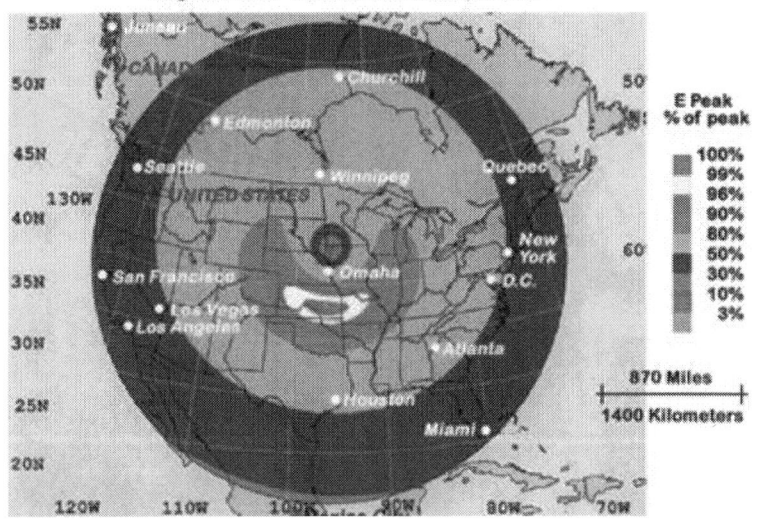

Illustration of EMP impact on United States, Canada, and Mexico if detonation occurred 298 miles above Nebraska. Retrieved from: https://www.bioprepper.com/2014/08/24/super-emp-capable-of-disabling-power-grid-across-lower-48-states/

Accurate strikes in these locations from varying altitudes would immediately bring US defense response and other capabilities in Alaska to its knees. In turn, a complete grid "black-out" would also likely bring about confusion, chaos, and eventual lawlessness impacting the effected populations of these areas.

A thermonuclear (EMP) mesospheric detonation over Anchorage would render all defensive capabilities inclusive of air, ground, communications, and Early Warning Detection/Response at Joint Base Elmendorf Richardson (JBER) and surrounding areas inoperable.

According to America's leading expert on EMPs, Dr. Peter V. Pry, even hardened military shelters in Alaska cannot withstand an EMP blast exceeding 50 kilovolts/meter.[7] Dr. Pry states that, "Russian Super-EMP weapons are

---

[7] This information was obtained in a recently published paper, *"Upgrading our Arctic Defenses,"* by Alaskan Ric Davidge. Dr. Peter Vincent Pry is a reviewer and resource of Mr. Davidge's paper and is quoted extensively in the paper. Dr. Pry is

designed to generate 200 kilovolts/meter" which, if reports are correct, lay far beyond any current EMP protection capability the US military in Alaska maintains.

A thermonuclear (Super-EMP) mesospheric detonation over Nenana would be much more devastating to US defense capability. This would render all defense capabilities (Air, Ground, Communications, Early Warning Detection, and Missile Response) at Clear Air Station, Ft. Wainwright, and Eielson Air Base inoperable. Though missile intercepts could be possible if launched immediately, it is highly unlikely that actual intercepts would transpire based on historical testing, as well as unknown testing, against the Club-K at low altitudes.[8]

In addition to this, the now operational hypersonic missile capability maintained by both Russia and China would be nearly unstoppable, if even detected, before striking their targets over Alaska. There would be virtually no missile response capability to defend Alaska in the case of hypersonic missile implementation. No air capabilities to defend against any incursion into Alaska, no way to move troops, and no communications available to the outside world with the exception of Ft. Greely if it were still operationally capable. A near complete communications black-out across Alaska would

---

the Executive Director of the Task Force on National and Homeland Security, a Congressional Advisory Board dedicated to achieving protection of the United States from electromagnetic pulse (EMP), cyber-attack, mass destruction terrorism and other threats to civilian critical infrastructure on an accelerated basis as well as being the Director of the United States Nuclear Strategy Forum. Dr. Pry was an intelligence officer with the Central Intelligence Agency responsible for analyzing Soviet and Russian nuclear strategy, operational plans, military doctrine, threat perceptions, and developing U.S. paradigms for strategic warning (1985-1995). He also served as a verification analyst at the U.S. Arms Control and Disarmament Agency responsible for assessing Soviet compliance with strategic and military arms control treaties (1984-1985). Retrieved at:
https://secureservercdn.net/198.71.233.47/n5q.11d.myftpupload.com/wp-content/uploads/2020/08/8_6_20-Upgrading-our-Arctic-Defenses-.pdf

[8] Information obtained at https://en.wikipedia.org/wiki/Ground-Based_Midcourse_Defense#Intercept_tests and https://en.wikipedia.org/wiki/Fort_Greely#North_Korea_missile_defense suggests that no current US capability is recorded for intercept against the low altitude flight capability of the Club-K.

transpire. This information is again based on Dr. Pry's expertise as quoted in Mr. Davidge's paper.

A thermonuclear (Super-EMP) stratospheric detonation over Kodiak would render all Coast Guard defense capabilities there (Air, Sea, and Communications) inoperable, completely cut-off from Anchorage, JBER, and potentially North America.

An alternative consideration to EMP detonations over Alaska would be that of either cyber-attack or targeted sabotage operations conducted against the Alaska based power-grid. An attack of this type would not be as detrimental to US forces in Alaska as related to defense response and capability. Attacks of these types would specifically target the population and critical infrastructure necessary to sustain societal normalcy which provides for basic necessities such as water and electricity to name but two. It is believed that both cyber-attacks and coordinated sabotage attacks on the power-grid of Alaska would be conducted in order to generate mass confusion amongst the population which would indirectly impact military capability and response.

The chaos that would transpire after either an EMP, cyber-attack, or targeted sabotage operations directly impacting the population and critical infrastructure will be discussed more in-depth in the following Chapter. However, it would be highly probable that adversary forces would strategically plan for, and capitalize on, the internal conflict and chaos in larger Alaskan cities that would arise from the population towards its governing authorities and eventually, towards each other.

Elimination of Coastal EWD Capabilities

External threat operations to eliminate coastal EWD capabilities (radar sites) will also likely commence either just before or near immediately after the targeted critical infrastructure strikes internally. This portion of Phase I will include selective targeting of both military and civilian radar sites ranging from Kaktovik to Shemya Island and some further inland. Radar sites could be eliminated by surface launched Club-K missiles armed with high-explosive warheads or by multi-role Russian and/or Chinese attack aircraft. With the near immediate elimination of these sites, NORAD/NORTHCOM will be rendered blind along much of the western Alaska coastal region with the exception of possible dedicated satellite coverage which could also be tremendously hindered by inclement weather or cloud coverage[9] if the Russians and Chinese utilized these factors in their strategic planning.

Phase II

Phase II involves gaining air superiority over much of the area in the northwestern portions of Alaska as illustrated in the following figure. Everything west of the Nulato Hills and north of the Ray Mountains will necessitate adversarial air superiority for Phase II initiation and completion. Air superiority will initially include both Russian and/or Chinese multi-role fighter and close air support aircraft. If air superiority is achieved by foreign forces, responses to these areas will be minimal by US aircraft currently stationed in Alaska, Thule, or Canada.

In looking at the illustration, it is noticed that the mostly likely areas of interest for a foreign adversary lie west, northwest, and north of all prominent military facilities with key natural terrain obstacles protecting potential areas of operation. These key obstacles serve as a "buffer" against internal projection of US or NATO forces and, when combined with additional weather and climate factors as described in current Arctic Strategy, makes it easily defendable by air, ground, and sea.

In combination with the air superiority campaign will be the strategic bombing of targets already "softened" as a result of the EMP strikes. Bombers, accompanied by fighter aircraft, will provide strikes deep within the Alaskan interior and Alaskan southeast on specified targets near, in, and outside of Fairbanks and Anchorage. These targets would include Clear Air Station, Eielson Air Base, Ft. Wainwright, Ft. Greely, Joint Base Elmendorf Richardson, Fairbanks International Airport, and Ted Stevens International Airport in Anchorage. Additionally, many roadways, railways, bridges, ports, and other critical infrastructure will also be targeted.

---

[9] Inclement weather and cloud coverage could obstruct US satellite visibility capability as is noted in the Department of the Air Force Arctic Strategy.

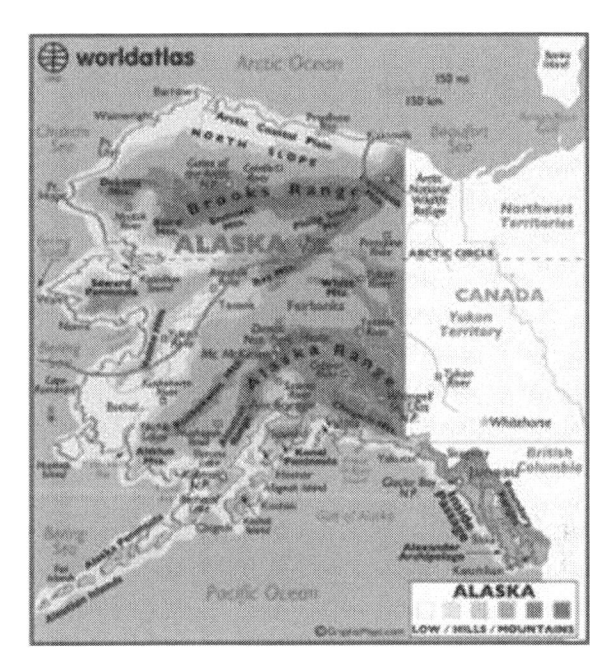

Air superiority must be gained by occupation forces in the skies of western Alaska. Retrieved online at: https:// www.worldatlas.com/maps/united-states/alaska. Amended with "red line" across the State by the author.

These bombing strikes will be conducted so as to prevent immediate response by US forces in Alaska, to destroy any immediate capability for reinforcement by US or Allied forces in accordance with the Order of Battle, and to incite chaos and fear amongst the population. Any US aircraft that were able to take to the skies will quickly be brought down due to being significantly outnumbered by the fighter aircraft accompanying the enemy bombers. It would be a matter of attrition.

Once air superiority is achieved west of the Nulato Hills and over Nome, Russian and/or Chinese Airborne forces will be inserted in order to immediately seize Nome and its airfield. With close air support being provided to aid in suppression of early localized resistance efforts, Airborne forces should be able to either jump directly over the airfield (or nearby if necessary), be inserted via helicopter air assault from ships in the Strait, or simply land in Nome with their equipment.

Upon securing the airfield, smaller units of Airborne forces will move immediately to seize the port. Wikipedia states that, "Russian Airborne Forces are well known for their mobility, utilizing a large amount of specifically designed vehicles built for airborne transport, as such, they are fully mechanized and traditionally have a larger complement of heavy weaponry than most contemporary airborne forces." This statement in Wikipedia is supported by the Defense Intelligence Agency publication, *"Russia Military Power Report 2017"* (p. 55).[10] It would be more probable that combined Russian and Chinese Naval or Special Forces could also conduct a simultaneous assault (inserting from either a surface ship or submarine off the coast) and push inward from the sea to seize the port while Airborne forces focus their efforts on securing the town and seizing and securing the airport.

Phase III

With both the port and airport under the control of foreign military forces and communications cut due to EMP strikes elsewhere in Alaska, additional Airborne forces will turn their focus to quell any immediate local armed resistance and apprehend local leadership. In short-order, Nome falls. The Russian/Chinese alliance then lays claim to the Bering Strait due to having established military operational control over the entire area on both sides of the Strait. As a result, the Russians and Chinese now control the major global shipping lane to the Arctic via their effective blockade of the Strait and establishment of the Northern Sea Route.

Combined reinforcements inclusive of troops, equipment, helicopter assets, armor assets, mobile air defense (MANPADs), semi-permanent air defense emplacements, fuel, etc. begin arriving by military airlift and seaborne vessels from the Bering Strait and across the corridor. A Russian/Chinese foothold on US soil has now been established complete with Command and Control (C2) elements, troops for security, an airfield from which to receive critical resupply, launch offensive operations, and air defense capabilities to protect their assets. This portion of Phase III will also demonstrate a "slowing" of the

---

[10] More on Russian Airborne forces and capabilities is available in the Defense Intelligence Agency publication mentioned above.

campaign in order to properly secure and stabilize the foothold in Nome. As discussed, this intentional "slowing" allows for advancement of logistical resupply, reinforcement, and air defense capability emplacements in order to protect assets and prevent over-reach in obtaining their farther strategic objectives too quickly. The slowing also provides time to add additional fortification measures to their foothold.

Phase IV

During the slowing of the campaign in Nome, population containment operations also begin. "Specialists" in counterinsurgency operations will be brought in so as to gain and maintain the immediate control of the population *before* resistance efforts have the opportunity to become active, and prior to developing the means to resist.

It is believed that these specialists will utilize a "heavy-handed" approach (based on the COIN Authoritarian Model) in order to effectively contain the population and immediately break their will. COIN operations will also likely be utilized by the Russians and Chinese in accordance with lessons learned in previous geographical locations/campaigns which *will include* considerations of potential exposure to any biological weapon that may have been previously released and the local population exposure. Strict consideration will be taken as to how local conditions associated with any biological weaponry which might have been utilized may impact operations and sustainment of their own forces in the immediate and long term. The use of biological weapons is unlikely however, the possibility should be considered.

The counterinsurgency effort implemented will be designed in order to immediately crush the will of the people to resist. This will include "active" measures taken in attempts to force the population into submission. The earlier this goal is achieved in Nome, the better for the Russians and/or Chinese to pursue additional strategic goals and interests. After settling in, expansion of the area of operations begins in North and North-eastward directions, along the coastal areas, to include air defense asset emplacement and establishment of forward patrol bases and helicopter capable landing zones.

Helicopter-borne/Air assault and riverine operations (via dog teams or snowmachines if needed during the winter) will be utilized to expand the occupied area in order to reach difficult objectives such as the trans-Alaska pipeline. These operations initially target coastal and inland communities maintaining critical infrastructure assets (airports/airfields, small ports, refueling capabilities, etc.) needed by combined external threat forces. Close air support is provided for operations via a newly established "air base" in Nome as well as sea-borne aircraft along the coast. These operations will "leap-frog" one another while maintaining the ability to move logistical assets into secured areas once stabilized. The primary concern of occupying forces is not to move farther or faster than near immediate reinforcement, resupply, and close air support will allow. Once new communities fall under occupied control, additional security and counterinsurgency methods are implemented similar to those in Nome.

Closing

The previous scenario was not developed by inputting data into a computer; this was not a scenario of technological war-gamming. It was also not developed to illustrate the strength of the US military, US leadership, or how easily US forces could repel foreign invaders from Alaska or the Arctic Region because, simply put, strength of US Arctic forces does not exist. This scenario was developed through extensive historic information obtained through open-source research in order to illustrate how a well-trained, a well-equipped, and an exceptionally well-prepared combined Russian/Chinese Arctic military force could invade Alaska. This scenario is conceivable due to two decades of neglect in the region by many US politicians, many in the US military, and the fact that our adversaries have been training and preparing for war in the Arctic.

Although the DOD and its military services have now provided multiple strategies and defined what must be done within the context of their writings, there remains stagnant implementation combined with vastly archaic defense systems and equipment loosely defending Alaska. This fact is in conjunction with ill-prepared forces already stationed in Alaska which might very well find themselves directly involved in conflict in an Arctic environment there or abroad.

If this scenario (or one similar) happened, it is imperative that Russian and/or Chinese forces protect their established foothold and expand their area of operations and influence from that location. It simply cannot be permitted that once in Alaska, forces from the US and other NATO countries drive the occupiers back into, and across, the Bering Strait. Nome and similar communities must be protected at all costs by the invaders, and it is believed that the local population there will be utilized in doing so (use your imagination). As well, it must also be considered as to what might occur if the adversary were driven back. Would they completely destroy existing critical infrastructure in their retreat? Would they resort to utilizing small-scale nuclear weapons after their withdrawal? Would they risk a global nuclear war to "save face" in the international community?

As portrayed in the scenario, it is a relatively short-period of time of the invasion that the population of Alaska in several locations could potentially be experiencing a total black-out due to the EMP detonations, cyber-attack, or targeted sabotage attacks on critical infrastructure. No cell phones or computers, no electricity, no water, no sewage or trash removal capability, possibly no mechanized mode of transportation, no way to shop for groceries or essential items, no debit or credit card transactions, and no news sources. The population will not know exactly what had transpired although many would witness the strategic bombing of critical targets by the Russians and Chinese and many might be killed as a result of collateral damage.

For the scenario provided, the people of Nome will be cut-off from any military response and desperately needed assistance. When will US forces be able to respond to what has taken place? It is proposed that it would take the US forces in Alaska several days to mount any type of <u>effective</u> military response to an occupation of Nome. Provided that an occupation could be the situation encountered, the people have only two choices: submit or resist.

Chapter 4

Ensuing Chaos

In locations impacted by either an EMP, cyber-attack, or sabotage of critical infrastructure, law and order will eventually surrender to chaos. The chaos will also impact other surrounding communities as well due to "spillage." It is strongly believed that the disruption to the daily lives and the absence of basic needs requirements of thousands of people across Alaska will play to the advantage of the Russian and/or Chinese strategic plan.

Lawlessness, or at least elevated levels of civil disobedience, exhibited by the population will eventually transpire when governance can no longer enforce the law or meet the basic needs of the population. When governance no longer has the means to effectively govern, the population will first turn *on* governance, and then, on each other. This is historical fact that we have seen play out in Iraq, Afghanistan, and many other places globally. Would the America population be so different under the same circumstances? I believe that we like to think that we would. However, common sense tells me that a population's desire to survive, even by any means necessary under dire circumstances, would quickly override any proud misconceptions that may currently be held.

Creation of internal discord in/around major metropolitan areas of Alaska will be advantageous to foreign forces as conflict between the population and governance, and then the population and population, will work in tandem with the difficulty that American forces will be facing in being able to project forces internally across the State. It would be highly probable, near immediately after any of these attacks, that the active component US forces stationed in Alaska would be immediately called to, and secured in the confines of, their nearest base.

The Alaska National Guard and other organized militia forces of the State would also be activated but then a logical question arises. Would those members choose to answer the call and report for duty, or would they stay home in order to protect their own families? It is my belief that the National Guard response would be minimal. My assertion is based on historically documented facts associated with the COVID-19 pandemic and the Alaska

National Guard response during that time. It is believed that most National Guard personnel, who have thought well in advance of a situation such as this happening in Alaska, would choose to remain at home and protect their families and I certainly would not be one to blame them. I strongly believe that a great number of people here in Alaska, especially those living well outside of metropolitan areas (and even many within), would choose to "bug in" and stay home to protect their families from internal dangers over that of leaving their families in order to protect their State and/or their country. What I have previously stated does not imply, by any means, that those who do not choose to "answer the call" to protect their State and country are selfish or that they are cowards. Rather, it implies that Maslow's Hierarchy of Needs would subconsciously, and consciously, come into play for everyone affected.

It can be seen in the following illustration that everyone has the same needs, whether realized or not. The most immediate of which, as described by Maslow, are those found in the bottom three portions of the pyramid. In order of priority, they are: 1). Psychological Needs, 2). Safety Needs, and 3). Love and Belonging Needs. The people will both consciously and subconsciously revert to a purely survival mode. Their preservation of self and family will be their top priority while any concern for the defense of State and/or country will appear far down their priority list if that concern even appears at all. Logically speaking, if chaos ensues and governance (local, State, and Federal) cannot meet the basic needs of the population (i.e., water, food, electricity, safety, security, enforcement of law, etc.), then the people will take it upon themselves to find ways, means, and methods to meet those needs for themselves. Any trust in the Government will have deteriorated due to the fact that, as stated, governance can no longer meet the basic needs and requirements of the population. As we have seen in other places, such as Iraq and Afghanistan, the population will assume responsibility for their own safety, security, and well-being whenever governance fails to provide.

In the event of attacks targeting critical infrastructure, virtually everything could be rendered useless, especially from an EMP. No electricity means no way to utilize debit or credit cards as a means of purchasing needed items. Cash money will eventually become worthless paper. There will be no running water or wastewater utility services available. Food in refrigerators and freezers will spoil within hours. No gasoline or diesel fuel at the pumps can be obtained due to the pumps requiring electricity and their being controlled by the interior computer systems of the filling station or by the convenience store.

Maslow's Hierarchy of Needs pyramid. Retrieved from: www.simplypsychology.org/maslow.html

No heating fuel to be delivered because there is no way to pay. No cellphone service or internet, which means that communications would be extremely limited. There would be limited hospital access and capability. Any backup generators would eventually run out of fuel if they could run at all after an EMP attack. Emergency response capability for police, fire, and medical services will be near minimal because all radio communications capabilities will be non-existent. The system will be inundated, and some vehicles might cease to even function. The list of damage as a result of an attack like this is endless. *

*Note: I highly recommend watching National Geographic's *"American Blackout,"* the approximately 47-minute video *"New York News Coverage of the Northeast Blackout of 2003"*, and *"Lights Out: The Danger to the US Power Grid"* to gain a far better understanding of what is likely to transpire in a prolonged, grid-down situation. All of these videos can be found on YouTube.

Some might say, "Well, at least the Police are still out and about, and the National Guard has been deployed so that makes me feel safe." But what happens when the Police and the National Guard are no longer being paid during a prolonged black-out situation and they themselves begin experiencing the same problems with getting much-needed supplies (food and water) for their own families? Should it be *expected* that their sense of patriotism and defense of their country or community will be placed above their personal needs of self-preservation and preservation of their own families?

To answer these questions, refer back to Maslow's Hierarchy of Needs. Does the pyramid mention anything about patriotism or defense of country or community? Eventually, the very people who were initially providing safety and security for the population will have no choice but to walk away from their posts in order to provide for, and protect, their own families. What happens then? An even greater descent into lawlessness and chaos.

Numerous sources available online have estimated that two-thirds to 90% of the population would die within a year after an EMP attack or a prolonged grid-down, black-out such as one that could be caused by a cyber-attack or sabotage. Causes of death during the first days and weeks alone could result from anything. Hunger/starvation, lack of water, social disruption, not being able to obtain required medications, communicable disease or illness, lack of regular medical treatment, hot and cold weather-related deaths, looting, rioting, robbery, and murder. Now, compound all of these potential causes of death with the fact that like-minded people will find each other and form groups (also in accordance with Maslow's Hierarchy). There will be active roving gangs and other criminal elements due to the near total absence of law enforcement. As a result of the increased level of criminal activity, vigilante groups and/or community security forces will form out of necessity for the safety and security of their communities. Make no mistake however, all will re-define the term "hunter/gatherer" in order to survive.

It is probable that FEMA will arrive, and encampments will be erected. But by the time FEMA arrives, civil discord and lawlessness will already have taken a firm hold across much of the population. It might very well be that martial law could be declared early, or near immediately, after a confirmed attack of any type; however, the implementation of martial law is a tremendous error in judgement on the part of governance. Why? Well, we all went through the "lockdowns" during the COVID crisis and saw how the population began to react after they finally woke-up to what was being imposed on them by the government "in the best interest of the population." Due to lessons harshly learned during the COVID lockdowns, I suspect that the population will immediately resist the employment of martial law or other types of restrictions. It will be more likely that any imposed restrictions on the population will serve to cultivate resentment and resistance *against* governance and the rule of law instead of broadening support for either. What could potentially transpire is the birth of countless numbers of what David Kilcullen has termed the "accidental guerrilla" who will stand unified in defiance and violent opposition of governance. Yet, any unity of these groups will eventually dissolve, causing a dangerous "splintering" of factions with all vying for the same thing...establishment of power and control and their version of governance.

As applied to the US Arctic Strategy and Homeland Defense, internal strife and conflict amongst the population will be created by our adversaries should they achieve success in targeting critical infrastructure. As was stated at the beginning of this Chapter, when governance cannot meet the basic needs of the population, then the population will turn on governance. If the response of governance is that of a "heavy handed" approach to restore order and maintain the rule of law, the population will respond accordingly. I personally would factor in the intentional creation of internal conflict between the population and governance as a part of my strategic planning. If I would do so, then why would the Russians and Chinese not plan for the same?

An internal conflict in major metropolitan cities and surrounding areas between the population and governance, or between the population and US military forces, on Alaskan soil will tremendously aid the efforts of adversarial occupation forces. This possibility could very well be an unanticipated and integral part of overall strategy by both the Russians and Chinese in the US Arctic region. There already exists the historical strain (over the past two and a half years alone) on the threads that are currently holding our Republic together. Many of those threads are highly worn and tremendously frayed which implies that the right amount of exerted pressure would cause many of them to completely break. What better way to aid in the occupation of Alaska than to have US forces actively engaged in a "counterinsurgency" effort against their own people while simultaneously having to conduct operations against the occupation forces? It would technically be a war on two fronts, and it is a part of adversarial strategy to consider.

Chapter 5

The Asymmetric Arctic Environment

The Arctic environment is already one of remarkable asymmetry due the harshness of its very nature. The terrain, the climate, and the near unpredictability of its weather are all attributes of the Arctic that make it tremendously harsh. All of these characteristics can prove advantageous and disadvantageous to both friendly and adversarial forces alike if carefully, or rather not carefully, planned for strategically. While moderate discussions of the Arctic climate and other environmental conditions have been made in existing strategies, other considerations of the Arctic environment have been omitted. The outward appearances of the current US Arctic Strategies have foregone critical considerations and in turn, the strategies project an illogical and limited approach related to warfare in such an environment.

It should be recognized that conflict in any Arctic environment will necessitate UW tactics. Tactics utilized by a guerrilla or resistance force, either directly (overt) or indirectly (covert) against the adversary, must be inclusive of UW concepts and planning that can be applied in the Arctic. An excellent example of UW concepts being utilized is revealed in examination of Finland's Winter War with the Soviets during 1939-1940. Though significantly outnumbered by the Soviet forces during the entire engagement, the Finn's employed asymmetric/guerrilla methods which provided them with countless tactical advantages. Advantages that in turn stalled the Soviet invasion for 105 days.

Tactics employed by the Finn's proved extremely costly to the inadequately prepared Red Army forces operating in the harsh environment. Historical data obtained reveals that the Soviets suffered 126,875 dead or missing, 264,908 wounded, and 5,600 captured[11] during the 105-day conflict. In addition, the Finn's strategic utilization of the extremely cold temperatures of -40 degrees Celsius also became advantageous to their fight. "Russian Soldiers had challenges with clothing, frozen weapons, too little food, and malfunctioning engines" (Raftsjo, 2018). In conjunction with Raftsjo, Dr.

---

[11] Data obtained from the article "The Winter War" written by Kennedy Hickman, 3 April 2019.

Paasi Tuunainen states that, "Winter reduces mobility, visibility, and the ease of doing mundane tasks such as drinking water or going to the toilet. At the same time, winter increases the need for equipment, food, and survival skills." These are all lessons which have been learned under the most difficult of circumstances by the Russians about Arctic warfare. Unfortunately, these are lessons which are only now being learned at the Northern Warfare Training Center in Black Rapids, Alaska by US forces who attend the courses there.

There should be extraordinarily little doubt posed by US planners that the lessons learned in Finland decades ago have been extensively studied and utilized specifically for the development of Arctic warfare tactics, techniques, training, and equipping of Russian units now positioned in the Russian Arctic. US forces cannot claim the same experiences or "learning curve" therefore, the implementation of UW to off-set the Russia advantage in an Arctic environment is necessary.

It has been assessed that current US Arctic Homeland Defense readiness and capability is inadequate and will be for years to come. This assessment should come as no surprise as the lack of readiness, capability, and effectiveness has been publicly presented in multiple forums and documents by the DOD. Even if it were possible to immediately implement all facets of existing Arctic Strategy by US forces today, there would remain a tremendous "gap" between current adversarial and US capability to operate *effectively* in the Arctic. To put things bluntly, our adversaries have a tremendous advantage in the Arctic operational environment because they actively train and prepare for extended operations there.

There are two primary reasons associated with the Russian advantage of effectively operating in the Arctic environment. They are:

1.) Our Russian adversaries are trained and have adapted their equipment and tactics specifically for winter warfare in the Arctic. And,

2.) The lack of US capability is due to the fact that the bulk of US forces are neither physiologically nor psychologically acclimated to the environment, they are not appropriately equipped, and they are not even moderately experienced for any prolonged operational effectiveness in austere Arctic conditions, particularly in the winter months.

In a December 2018 article in *Stars and Stripes,* it was reported that even troops stationed in both Alaska and Germany frequently suffered from cold-weather injuries such as hypothermia, chilblains, frostbite, and trench foot. Bringing in unacclimated forces from any of the lower 48 States to a harsh Arctic environment will, in all probability, result in an even higher number of cold-weather injuries, and even deaths, than the number typically expected. These types of injuries, as well as others suffered during warmer months, impact sustainment of the force and operations, not to mention the effect on morale. This speculation should have been effectively gauged in the Arctic Eagle exercise conducted in February 2022 as the need to "capture" this type of information is critical.

Grimly preceding the article regarding injuries in Alaska and Germany, and reinforcing the subject as well, is a February 1989 article by UPI. The UPI article exposed the extent of cold-weather injuries suffered by 253 of some 26,000 service members during a two-week exercise in Alaska known as "Brim Frost." Additional information reported in this article was that nine personnel also lost their lives in a C-130 crash landing during a dense ice fog at -52 below zero at Ft. Wainwright and of 590 fighter sorties scheduled for F-15s and other aircraft, only 143 were flown due to the impact of "bad weather" as reported.

UPI also reported, as related to the weather wreaking havoc on the exercise, that "Some of the critical site defense activity was cancelled because of low temperatures" and, "Our ground forces were in areas where the wind chill reached -120. On the average, most of them were sitting in areas between -50 and -75." Astonishingly, even after all the statistical data and factual information directly associated with Exercise Brim Frost presented otherwise, then Air Force LTG Thomas McInerney boastfully claimed success and having "whipped the weather" during one of Alaska's worst winters historically recorded at that time. Of course, this statement is easy to make from the warm confines of the Tactical Operations Center or a cozy office setting I suppose.

Undoubtedly, LTG McInerney's statement is one of tremendous denial. The probability of moving forward in Arctic military readiness, capability, and effectiveness with a mindset such as his, and countless others in the modern era, is very unlikely. However, LTG McInerney's statement provided many years ago has shed some light on a major concern that directly impacts Arctic military readiness, capability, and effectiveness of the force. The major concern now brought forth, albeit inadvertently, is that of Arctic Medicine and Medical Capability.

Arctic Medicine and Medical Capability

In the Spring 2023 article, *"Medical Support to the DoD Arctic Strategy,"* published in "AEther: A Journal of Strategic Airpower and Spacepower," US Air Force Lt. Col. Elizabeth Anne L. Hoettels honestly and factually presents Arctic Medicine and Capability issues associated with Arctic Warfare and current DOD Arctic Strategy. The shortcomings presented by Lt. Col. Hoettels directly bring to the forefront the impact on sustainment of the force, as well as conservation of the fighting strength, an Arctic environment will impose. In turn, the issues identified illustrate an additional problem as applied to the readiness, capability, and effectiveness of US forces in Alaska.

In her article, Lt. Col. Hoettels identifies many issues that are self-imposed and/or are absent from Arctic Strategy. Some of the issues identified by Hoettels, as directly quoted, are:

- *"While US Northern Command is the annex lead, no one individual, service, or command is orchestrating overall cold-weather medicine support efforts.*
- *Many service-specific Arctic medicine initiatives supporting the DOD strategy for the area of responsibility have not garnered input from the Alaska Command surgeon general or Alaska Air National Guard components—organizations that will be on the front lines should conflict arise.*
- *Local Alaskan civilians, the Indigenous tribal population, and coalition military partners with Arctic expertise are not included as participants in a meaningful way, in contravention of a vital aspect of the 2022 National Security Strategy— global alliances and strategic partnerships.*

47

- *Larger cold-weather military medicine structural issues exist as well. These challenges create unnecessary friction and confusion in this environment.*
- *The Departments of Defense and Homeland Security have varying levels of focus on cold-weather medicine.*
- *Resources are not being coordinated and consolidated to create a Joint cold-weather operational vision and capability.*
- *Individual services do not tie their ideas to the Joint Warfighting Concept during collaborative meetings as evidenced by the lack of critical stakeholders in their efforts."*

In applying the above identified issues to "Multidomain Operations" as extensively discussed in the October 2022 US Army Field Manual 3-0, *"Operations,"* on page 1-2, the immense relevance of Lt. Col. Hoettels' observations become overtly apparent. As Army FM 3-0 states:

"Multidomain operations are the combined arms employment of joint and Army capabilities to create and exploit relative advantages that achieve objectives, defeat enemy forces, and consolidate gains on behalf of joint force commanders. Employing Army and joint capabilities makes use of all available combat power from each domain to accomplish missions at least cost."

After identifying these issues, Lt. Col. Hoettels immediately makes a very profound follow-on statement:

"Without coordinated and integrated efforts focused on the same strategic problem, health services support in cold-weather operations may result in disjointed execution, impacting the US military's effective performance across all domains."

This statement by Lt. Col. Hoettels is astonishing and should serve as a "wake-up call" to military leadership across all Commands and the Pentagon, as well as to our NATO allies. The implications are that the operational readiness, capability, and effectiveness of US forces in the Arctic is unacceptably deficient and/or non-existent. As was previously stated in this book, the current US Arctic Strategy is a "Paper Tiger" and policy makers and military leadership continue to cultivate this less than honest narrative on a global stage.

UW Planning and Preparations

US planners must be realistic in their assessment of conducting Arctic warfare operations. As has now been provided with historical information, it is time to consider that Arctic operations must be inclusive of guerrilla warfare (i.e., UW) planning and preparations based on the indication that Indigenous knowledge of the environment is necessary.

Implementation of UW methodology must be utilized in an Arctic conflict, especially with the expectation of population engagement. Prior to the US implementing this methodology however, two questions should be posed by leadership:

1.) Has the US measured the risk vs. reward factor of RO in operational planning? And,

2.) Will the US impose on itself the same self-righteous positioning that it imposed on our enemies who utilized RO (guerrilla warfare) tactics against us in Vietnam, Iraq, and Afghanistan arguing specifically that the utilization of guerrilla warfare is unethical?

As related to the second question, I suspect that any existing ethical dilemma or reservations the USG or military might have in utilizing similar tactics will be dismissed with justification provided as the attempt to gain an advantage over such formidable adversaries like the Russians and Chinese. Is the US not actively engaged in supporting a guerrilla war by proxy, or to be more politically correct "Resistance Operations," currently in Ukraine? I ask, what tactics are the Ukrainian resistance members (the population) utilizing that are not being reported to the general public?

In the event of an Arctic conflict, RO will be primarily conducted by smaller units and/or individuals comprised mostly of the population. This assertion is factual and is in alignment with current UW doctrine and the ROC. Adding to this is the fact that hardships encountered associated with climate and other environmental conditions will impede larger conventional, and even

SOF, units from gaining access to denied areas. If Iraq and Afghanistan have proven anything, it is that larger conventional, and even unconventional, units will be confined for prolonged periods to the larger forward operational bases. In a manner of direct correlation, the larger bases of Iraq and Afghanistan would be equivalent to those currently located in Anchorage, Juneau, and Fairbanks. Due to weather and climate related hardships, operational capability (logistical, communications, flight operations, satellite capability, etc.) would be hindered, even nullified, as has been readily identified in current US Arctic Strategy.

To additionally note, any existing "Fulda Gap" mentality or approach to warfare in the Arctic should immediately be dismissed. This mentality, which unfortunately continues to be exhibited by many, indicates a complete lack of familiarity and understanding of Arctic terrain (during both winter and warmer months) which portrays a lack of fundamental understanding of historical lessons thus being an uneducated approach to potential conflict in the Arctic. The Arctic environment will require a non-traditional mindset, alternative approaches to problem solving, and indigenous knowledge for sheer survivability and war-fighting capability. The recognition of these factors outwardly exhibits the need for UW in the Arctic.

Chapter 6

Arctic Homeland Defense

"Arctic Homeland Defense (AHD) is a joint military force and USG interagency effort. SOF, particularly SF and Psychological Operations (PSYOP, now Information Operations) and Civil Affairs (CA) forces, are well suited to conduct or support AHD operations because these forces have unique functional skills inclusive of cultural and language training. SOF may conduct AHD in the absence of any other military efforts (Federal or State), support other ongoing military or civilian assistance efforts, or support the employment of conventional forces in promoting AHD strategy."

(Extracted from *FM 3-05.202, Special Forces Foreign Internal Defense Operations, Ch. 1, Para. 1, p. 1-1* and modified for application to Arctic Homeland Defense.)

To put things in a bit of a different context, AHD operations in Alaska should be planned and prepared for, conducted, and exercised in order to not only strengthen homeland defense, but to also engage with the population in order to acquire their support and invaluable knowledge of the environment. Operations and exercises such as these can assist in positively shaping the operational environment of remote areas.

Domain Awareness and Sovereignty Assurance - IDAD

AKOM Forces in the Arctic

It is stated in the Department of the Air Force's Arctic Strategy 2020 that, *"The Arctic represents a cornerstone of the nation's defense."* This statement is more a partial truth in that prior to laying any cornerstone, the all-important aspect of a solid foundation must be present. In conjunction with a strong and level foundation, and the initial laying of the cornerstone and all stones that follow, there must also exist a quality mortar to bind it together. In this case, the "mortar" consists of the personnel who constitute the Alaska Organized Militia (AKOM). If the Air Force stands by its own statement, then it could be logically argued that Alaska is the very foundation on which *the* cornerstone of our nation's defense rests in the Arctic Region.

It is well known that Alaska (and the Arctic) is one of the harshest environments on the planet that is comprised of some of the most inaccessible, inhospitable, and humanly uninhabitable areas found anywhere. These facts are clearly recognized and supported in the contents of the Air Force Arctic Strategy section pertaining to "The Changing Strategic Environment." However, there is a factor that continues to remain of little consideration in all existing strategies. This factor is that of the people who live there.

The personnel of AKOM stand ready to provide existing Arctic strategies with uniquely tremendous advantages yet, they oft remain overlooked in the scheme of more grandiose strategic ideology and policy making. AKOM forces in the Arctic are, in many aspects, the first line of our National and Homeland Defense in the region. An example of AKOM providing an advantage to Arctic Strategy is the ability to conduct domain awareness and community vulnerability assessments in remote/strategic locations when/where active component forces cannot. The Air Force Strategy (p. 11) states:

"Interoperability is especially critical in the Arctic region due to terrain, limited access, and the low-density of domain awareness assets."

This is a knowledge "gap" identified in the Air Force strategy. Another especially important statement (p. 13) of the strategy states,

"To ensure readiness, the Air and Space Forces must prepare for increased activity in the region and practice jointly and multi-nationally, learning from allies and partners."

AKOM elements are indeed partners in the "One Team, One Fight" concept and other US forces stationed in Alaska (as well as those who might find themselves deployed there) should be seeking to actively train with, and learn from, AKOM personnel who call Alaska their home.

A unique capability which AKOM can provide to overall strategy is that of "outside the box" conduction of operations with the permissible latitude necessary to accomplish tremendously difficult missions. Such an example is the use of dogsled teams and snowmobiles which are frequently utilized in many areas of Alaska during winter months for mobility, supply and re-supply, search and rescue, and access between villages or communities. These forms of transportation and logistical support are of such importance, that the Russian military has been conducting training for several years in their utilization and potentially effective tactical employment (in conjunction with reindeer/caribou team methods). US military forces should also be exploring these methods as well. Dogsled teams and snowmobile capabilities are numerous in Alaska with many AKOM personnel either owning these assets or having direct contact with people who utilize these resources for transportation or subsistence annually.

Russian military dogsled team, 2016. (Retrieved from https://defence-blog.com/news/army/russian-soldiers-go-native-for-arctic-ops-using-reindeer-and-dogsleds.html).

Russian military with reindeer team, 2016. (Retrieved from https://defence-blog.com/news/army/russian-soldiers-go-native-for-arctic-ops-using-reindeer-and-dogsleds.html).

Mao Zedong once said, *"The guerrilla must move amongst the people as a fish swims in the sea."* While AKOM personnel are not guerrillas, they would find themselves heavily involved in RO therefore the overall sentiment of Mao's statement does apply. A smaller force of AKOM personnel from the Alaska State Defense Force (ASDF) can blend immediately with the population of nearly any given area of Alaska with far less effort than a larger conventional force or even a smaller unconventional team. This fact is especially true in remote villages and communities of Alaska. Smaller units or detachments of AKOM personnel with capabilities associated primarily with domain awareness patrolling and security could also be utilized as a very much needed intelligence collection, surveillance, and reconnaissance asset when necessary.

Having a reduced unit size (military "footprint") in conjunction with local language skills (Alaskan Native languages) and cultural understanding, combined with profound knowledge of specific geographical areas where they operate, would be beneficial to all aspects of US Arctic Strategy. Familial, and tribal ties with the Native community across the area, along with relaxed grooming standards in order to blend with the population, would allow operations to be conducted without drawing unwanted attention by foreign occupation forces. With the ability to blend with the population, operations involving gathering and dissemination of critical intelligence on foreign forces operating in the occupied areas could be possible. This is a UW methodology designed for force multiplication which provides advantages at all levels.

AKOM Leadership

AKOM in Alaska is composed of the Alaska Air and Army National Guard, the ASDF, and the Alaska Naval Militia (ANM). All entities are legitimately recognized by the Alaska Department of Military and Veterans Affairs (DMVA) and are under command of the Alaska Adjutant General (TAG) and the Governor. As legitimately recognized entities, the DOD, the Alaska Governor, the TAG, and the Joint Staffs of AKOM and ALCOM must be encouraged to value the necessity and capabilities of these forces as they relate to AHD *and* as they apply to Arctic Strategy. However, there are at least a few people in the Alaska DMVA, and even others in the State legislature, who would like to see the ASDF completely dissolved. The knowledge of this fact is very alarming. Why would anyone at the State level want to see a homeland defense capability in Alaska done away with? This simply is not logical.

To date, the State of Alaska has only moderately developed an Alaska Arctic Strategy specific to AKOM. The developed strategy minimally supports existing DOD military strategies pertaining to the Arctic which is to say that it was done in order for the "boxes" to be checked. This is an identified deficiency in AHD that must be corrected. In conjunction with this, there exists a lack of implementation of appropriate measures to protect the homeland through *deterrence* in the Alaskan Arctic Region. Absence of deterrence serves as an enabling action for adversarial incursions into the US homeland as was an occurrence that quietly took place on the North Slope in 2020. Deterring our adversaries is the third defense objective noted in the 2018 National Defense Strategy. However, the focus on domestic emergency response operations in Alaska has seemingly taken priority over those of National Defense. This fact can be logically deduced by reading the State of Alaska's Emergency Operations manual. With all of these combined elements, it is easy to interpret that State of Alaska leadership at all levels have turned a "blind eye" to deterring our adversaries and the defense of the US Homeland in Alaska.

State of Alaska leadership must become far more proactive and attentive to issues related to Homeland Defense. They should actively plan and exercise for the contingency of external threat incursion (which has already happened) of the State. In doing so, they must also prepare the State Emergency Operations Center to become the primary Command and Control element at the "forward edge" of the battlespace in the event that US forces in Alaska lost that capability. They must understand how to take a State asset and rapidly transition it into a National Defense asset in the event of this type of crisis.

Both the Governor and TAG must also become more proactive in forging relationships with active component military leadership positioned in the State as these relationships are currently near non-existent. It is <u>imperative</u> that both the Governor and TAG be directly involved in operational planning related to Arctic Strategy, Homeland Defense, and UW aspects which could possibly arise in Alaska. Should they choose not to be directly involved, someone from each of their respective offices should be assigned. If no one wants the job, then perhaps it is time for a change in State leadership. Complacent attitudes associated with US Arctic Strategy and Homeland Defense through America's Arctic must change as complacency will get many Alaskans killed.

Chapter 7

Challenges to the Defense of Alaska

Disclaimer: This Chapter is tremendously informative on a different level. It should be known that what is written was not taken from any classified source or material. All conclusions were derived from open-source information found in the public domain with additional information having been obtained from highly respected and credible sources who wish to remain anonymous.

What might be surprising to learn is that the State of Alaska currently lacks a comprehensive defense plan that exhibits a clear chain of command, integrated communications systems, and consistent domain awareness systems and assets inclusive of all military forces within the Alaska AO. These facts illustrate incredible vulnerabilities in Homeland Defense capability, operational readiness, and effectiveness.

The Director of National Intelligence (DNI) unclassified threat assessment of February 2022 states:

"Competition and potential conflict between nation-states remain a critical national security threat. Beijing, Moscow, Tehran, and Pyongyang have demonstrated the capability and intent to advance their interests at the expense of the United States and its allies. China increasingly is a near-peer competitor, challenging the United States in multiple arenas—especially economically, militarily, and technologically—and is pushing to change global norms and potentially threatening its neighbors. Russia is pushing back against Washington where it can—locally and globally—employing techniques up to and including the use of force."

To state it bluntly, the DNI threat assessment reflects increased levels of both capability and intent of our adversaries, as well as their objectives, to be gained at the expense of the United States.

Given what the DNI threat assessment states, it is plausible to ask ourselves a serious question. Are we prepared to meet these threats to the US homeland specifically in Alaska? While speculation of a classified plan to defend Alaska and North America does in all probability exist on a National level, it probably requires substantial improvement. This chapter will present what appears to be the absence of a combined or joint effort. Based on current knowledge presented below, any plan in existence would lack balance, synchronization, total forces integration and coordination, and has not been exercised holistically since the end of the Cold War. This is a major issue and concern for the US Arctic region.

The purpose of this chapter is to seize the attention of influencers, decision and policy makers, and military leadership in order to gain their support and advisement in synchronizing, coordinating, planning, and once again exercising the universal defense of Alaska which should be inclusive of all forces found within Alaska. The threat to the US homeland through an Alaska avenue of approach has increased dramatically within the last 24 months alone and an effort to improve the defense of Alaska is emergently warranted. Not to strongly advocate for such a homeland defense effort would be less than responsible. If we know these problems exist, both Russia and China know it as well.

The Problem

Alaska lies along the seam of three major commands and areas of operational responsibility (AOR). These major commands are the U.S Indo-Pacific Command (USINDOPACOM), U.S. Northern Command (USNORTHCOM), and the U.S. European Command (USEUCOM). In speaking from a historical perspective, the majority of coordinative responsibilities regarding the defense of Alaska lays somewhere between USINDOPACOM and USNORTHCOM. This relationship has been a challenge so this will be a focus in this chapter. Hopefully, those reading will find some potential solutions, methodologies, and answers to the challenges presented.

Through research of this topic, it appears that US Air Force unit missions in Alaska are more readily defined, coordinated, synchronized, and exercised than ground units within the same AOR. As taken from the Joint Base Elmendorf Richardson (JBER) website:

"The North American Aerospace Defense Command (NORAD) is a binational United States and Canadian organization charged with the missions of aerospace warning and aerospace control for North America. Aerospace warning includes the monitoring of manmade objects in space, and the detection, validation, and warning of attack against North America whether by aircraft, missiles, or space vehicles, utilizing mutual support arrangements with other commands. Aerospace control includes ensuring air sovereignty and air defense of the airspace of Canada and the United States. Alaskan NORAD Region is responsible for completing the NORAD mission within the State of Alaska and the surrounding waters."

Based on this mission statement one could conclude that domain awareness in the areas of air and space are well covered by NORAD in Alaska. Yet, there remains an unspecified genuine concern due to the lack of a standardized methodology used to communicate between commands. Most specifically impacted by this concern are NORAD, the 11th Airborne Division, and the Alaska National Guard (AKNG) Joint Staff (AKNGJS). This is not to exclude the US Navy (USN) and US Coast Guard (USCG) who are responsible for the "surrounding waters" per each individual branch published Arctic Strategy.

Outward appearances allude to there being no formal lines of communication between the multiple commands previously mentioned. Concurrently, there is no known current full time liaison officer (LNO) from the 11th Airborne Division, AKNGJS, US Navy North (NAVNORTH), or USCG posted in the Alaska Command Joint Operations Center (JOC). These identified positions are tremendously necessary to fill in order to "warn of attack" or "deploy ground or naval forces" to a potential scene or event.

In some cases, Alaska Army National Guard (AKARNG) forces, ASDF units, or the Alaska Naval Militia (ANM) could potentially be much closer to a ground or water event, scenario, or scene than could active-duty ground forces stationed at active-duty installations in Alaska. Alaska specific units (AKANG, ASDF, ANM) are better geographically located in many forward areas which aids in responding more rapidly given that many of these forces are stationed in some twenty communities off the Alaska road system.

One may argue to the contrary that the AKNGJS may be informed through informal relationships. While there does exist this possibility, potentially the NAVNORTH and USCG have neither known formalized coordinated efforts currently in existence between the multiple commands nor have they been exercised in combined joint homeland defense scenarios in decades.

The current Alaska Command (ALCOM) website states that:

"Alaskan Command, in coordination with trusted partners, conducts homeland defense, civil support, mission assurance, and security cooperation within the ALCOM Joint Operational Area (JOA) to defend and secure the United States and its interests. ALCOM is headquartered at Joint Base Elmendorf-Richardson, Alaska, and falls under U.S. Northern Command as a subordinate unified command. DoD forces in Alaska include more than 22,000 US Air Force, US Army, US Navy, and US Marine Corps personnel, and 4,700 Guardsmen and Reservists."

Portions of this statement are inaccurate and in turn, are misleading to the public. DOD forces in Alaska do include approximately 4,700 Guardsman however, they neither "fall under" USNORTHCOM nor ALCOM. So, to whom do they belong? The answer is shocking.

The ALCOM Commander has extremely limited ground forces for his use at any given time. The fact of the matter is that both the 11th Airborne Division and AKARNG forces are assigned to USINDOPACOM and more specifically, the US Army Pacific (USARPAC) Commander. Shocking huh? Currently, the ALCOM Commander neither commands nor controls, nor are ground forces assigned to (including AKARNG forces), ALCOM. The bottom line being that the ALCOM Commander has little to no influence over these Alaska based units. Does this make any sense at all to anyone?

If there were to be an incident in Alaska requiring the use of active component Army units stationed in Alaska, the ALCOM Commander would need to request permission through the USNORTHCOM Commander to the USINDOPACOM Commander for a command relationship to be established with units stationed in Alaska. Similarly, the AKNG, while in a Title 32 status, belongs to the Governor of Alaska and the Adjutant General (TAG) of Alaska. If the ALCOM Commander wished to utilize any AKNG unit or units, it would require a similar request procedure. This relationship would change when AKNG forces were brought on Title 10 orders with most being currently prepared to provide support to the USINDOPACOM through USARPAC Commander's efforts in his joint operations area. Should the ALCOM Commander request that the AKNG be activated, they would potentially be further assigned to the Joint Forces Land Component Commander (JFLCC). However, as it stands, who would be the JFLCC in such an event? Would it be the 11th Airborne Division Commander?

Specifically related to the 11th Airborne Division and missions associated, remarks were made by US Army Chief of Staff, General James McConville, during a phone conversation in June 2022 with reporters. This conversation occurred before the 11th Airborne Division activation ceremony also in June 2022 where McConville stated, "We expect them (the 11th Airborne Division) to be masters of their craft in Arctic war-fighting, in extreme cold weather, in mountainous and high-altitude terrain, and we expect them to develop innovative ways of operating in this environment." McConville also added that "the 11th Airborne Division will be under U.S. Indo-Pacific Command and will focus on threats such as North Korea, Russia and China." This is overtly depictive of the 11th Airborne Division having multiple roles to include wearing "dual hats" while serving Commanders of both USINDOPACOM and USNORTHCOM simultaneously. Major General Brian Eifler, the 11th Airborne Division Commander, commented in 2022 that, "Our mission is to deter the threats and be ready to fight and win both in the Indo-Pacific and the Arctic," with a follow-on statement of, 'And yes, that's a unique and difficult mission.'

An interesting part of General McConville's statement about the 11th Airborne Division that has gone un-noticed is that of, "*…we expect them to develop innovative ways of operating in this environment*" which provides for conduction of "outside the box" critical thinking. The latitude provided to MG Eifler by General McConville could potentially include preparation for, and implementation of, resistance operations and/or guerrilla warfare capability development.

11th Air Force's current mission statement from their website states:

"Provides combat ready forces for Commander Pacific Air Force (COMPACAF). Defends Alaska, Hawaii, and Guam and key strategic nodes against all threats. Deploys service component forces worldwide in response to major regional contingencies. Supports vital Pacific air bridge operation for throughput of strategic movement by contingency forces during crisis response. Provides support to federal and state authorities during civil emergencies, search, and rescue operations & counter narcotics interdictions."

So again, 11th Air Force units belong to USINDOPACOM and COMPACAF, not the USNORTHCOM Commander. This mission statement also includes "Defends Alaska..." as a portion of their mission which is encouraging however, as anyone can see, there exists a lot of "Red Tape" here.

Several Air Force units that conduct fulltime missions at JBER are actually Alaska Air National Guard (AKANG) units. One of which is the 176th Wing. Stating from their website:

"We conduct missions of Combat Search and Rescue, and Agile Combat Support for Air Expeditionary Force tasking, and Strategic Airlift, Homeland Defense, and Defense Support to Civil Authorities."

The 176th Wing is an AKANG unit that has remained relevant to the active-duty Air Force by absorbing a Title 10 Federal mission and has done well to have done so. A similar methodology or approach regarding an aligned active Army unit relationship available for the AKARNG should be considered given that the organization also participates in exercise "Arctic Edge" which *is* a Homeland Defense exercise.

Air Force units in Alaska share in portions of their various mission statements in that a part of what they do is "Defend Alaska." However, the question remains, to what extent do Air Force units exercise the defense of Alaska plan? During exercise "Red Flag," the exercises are designed to simulate a deployment to a contested environment where the battlefield strategy demands a high operational tempo and necessitates innovation, determination, and teamwork to stay ahead of ever-changing mission needs.

Many lessons learned during "Red Flag" are germane, however, the overall exercise is not specific to the defense of Alaska.

Exercise "Arctic Edge" is a biennial exercise which comes closest to an exercise to the defense of Alaska. As related to this exercise, it is stated:

"Arctic operations and exercises such as ARCTIC EDGE demonstrate the capabilities utilized to defend our homeland and our interests," said U.S. Air Force Lieutenant General David Krumm, Commander, Alaskan North American Aerospace Defense Command Region, North American Aerospace Defense Command; commander, Alaskan Command, U.S. Northern Command; and commander, 11th Air Force, Pacific Air Forces."

ARCTIC EDGE is a USNORTHCOM exercise scheduled every two years, first taking place in 2018. So, what forces participate in exercise Arctic Edge one might ask? From their website:

"ARCTIC EDGE 22 is linked to other service-specific exercises including the National Guard's ARCTIC EAGLE/PATRIOT, the U.S. Army's Joint Pacific Multinational Readiness Capability exercise and the U.S. Navy's ICE-X (Ice Exercise)."

Since LTG Krumm is the current ALCOM commander, having Air Force units participate is not a challenge. However, there remain many un-answered questions as to the participation of the Army, Marine, Navy, and Alaska National Guard. As can be seen thus far, many are generated from confusion. Of the more paramount questions are: If the ALCOM Commander has none of these forces or units in his command, how are other components forces participating in this exercise? What are the exercised command relationships? Who is the JFLCC? Is the 11th Airborne Division Commander assigned as the JFLCC? What does the 11th Airborne Division mission statement say? From their website, it is stated that the 11th Airborne Division website is currently under construction and will be operational shortly however, US Army Alaska's (USARAK) website states:

"United States Army Alaska provides trained and ready forces in support of worldwide unified land operations and supports United States Indo-Pacific Command Theater Security Cooperation Program in order to contribute to a

stable and secure operational environment. On order, executes Joint Force Land Component Command functions in support of Homeland Defense and Defense Support of Civil Authorities in Alaska."

So here again, Homeland Defense is espoused in the body of a mission statement, yet the fact remains that the presentation of "Homeland Defense" verbiage does not coincide with performance of such missions specifically related to the defense of Alaska. All of this is due primarily to obvious confusion which is overtly noticeable across the highest levels of command and from within the multiple commands themselves.

As of the last iteration of Arctic Edge, the USARAK Commander was designated as the JFLCC and it was observed that during the 2024 rotation of exercise Arctic Edge, the newly established 11th Airborne Division Commander will be designated as the JFLCC. However, it is unknown if this observation has been officially formalized in writing. Does/will the JFLCC have a relationship to the AKARNG during the exercise? The short answer is no in that no current command relationship exists between the JFLCC (11th ABN DIV Commander potentially) and the AKARNG. It has already been discussed that the AKARNG belongs to the USINDOPACOM and USARPAC Commander when on Title 10 orders and not the JFLCC in Alaska. This fact now brings forth the following questions:

1. Why are there no existing command relationships between the JFLCC and AKARNG?
2. Would the AKARNG be under the Operational Control (OPCON) of the JFLCC?
3. Would the AKARNG be under the Tactical Control (TACON) or could the AKARNG be assigned to the JFLCC as an organic unit?

Neither question 2 or 3 is currently known to have an answer nor has it been exercised in that the AKARNG, as once again stating, belongs to the USINDOPACOM and USARPAC Commander while on Title 10/Federal orders. This current status would allude to AKARNG personnel being deployed to the USINDOPACOM AOR, potentially Taiwan or Korea, in the event of a crisis in that geographical location.

From the AKARNG website:

"The Alaska Army National Guard is comprised of approximately 2,000 Guardsmen from more than 20 areas around the state. Our Guardsmen are trained and prepared to serve and protect the state of Alaska and the nation."

Following up on the previous point that Arctic Edge is a "linked exercise," including the National Guard's exercise 'Arctic Eagle/Patriot,' there is no answer provided as to *exactly how* they are linked given that it has been previously discussed that there is no command relationship.

To add even more confusion to an already confusing situation, former 29th Infantry Brigade Combat Team (IBCT) Commander, COL Moses Kaoiwi of the Hawaii Army National Guard (HIARNG), stated that, "the 1/297th Infantry (AKARNG) is tactically a subordinate unit to the 29th IBCT (HIARNG), though it (the 1/297 Infantry AKARNG) also reports to the Alaska Guard's 38th Troop Command." So, in short, the 29th IBCT of Hawaii is the higher headquarters for the largest ground force unit in the Alaska Army National Guard. How does this make sense logically or strategically for Homeland Defense in Alaska? Is it purely for geographical optics because Alaska could be a "projection platform" for forces into the Pacific?

In a related question, is the Arctic Eagle/Patriot exercise focused on Homeland Defense at all? According to the AKNG website:

"The exercise, conducted at JBER, Anchorage, Kodiak and Nome, is designed to increase the National Guard's capacity to operate in the Arctic and will pose <u>homeland security and state-level emergency scenarios</u> to facilitate realistic training in austere, extreme cold-weather environments across Alaska."

The answer to the previous question is a resounding "No." Their own website states that Arctic Eagle/Patriot is not a Homeland Defense exercise in any aspect. It is a <u>homeland security</u> exercise; therefore, this is neither an AKARNG Homeland Defense exercise nor is it an exercise based on defense at all. The AKARNG neither participates in an Alaska Homeland Defense specific exercise nor does it exercise a Homeland Defense plan representative of defending Alaska. This illustrates an incredible vulnerability gap in

Homeland Defense preparations and remains a missed opportunity to "train as we fight" as one unified team.

So, why then does the AKARNG not participate in Arctic Edge? If it is a matter of two separate exercise funding streams, then both should be combined with the alignment of exercises Arctic Edge and Arctic Eagle into a Homeland Defense and Homeland Security of Alaska exercise that includes both active and reserve components. Further, alignment and assignment of AKNG forces to the JFLCC *prior* to an event occurring in Alaska is of extreme importance. Transforming, developing, and reshaping portions of the AKARNG into the 3rd Brigade of the 11th Airborne Division would provide the best solution to organize these forces to fight and win for either USINDOPACOM or USNORTHCOM. This move would serve to enhance the capability of either combatant commander in most any given scenario.

It should also be stated that the USN's, USCG's, and US Marine Corps roles in the defense of Alaska (and the homeland through Alaska) should be clearly defined and integrated into both exercise and defense planning in accordance with DOD Arctic and Homeland Defense strategies. As it stands and has been illustrated, far too much confusion exists with each individual branch of service loosely following their own Arctic Strategy. All should instead be working towards the creation of a singular Joint Arctic Homeland Defense Strategy with the defense of Alaska at the core.

Recommendations to Rectify

Given the vast amount of information already presented in this chapter, there are some recommendations which can now be offered. They are:

1. As related to exercise and planning: Develop operational, contingency, and exercise plans that focus primarily on the defense of Alaska and include command relationships between all forces in Alaska (Active, National Guard, Reserve, Federal and State military forces inclusive of the ASDF and the ANM). Assure that exercises are conducted during winter months initially and after proficiency in winter warfare has been evaluated and achieved to standard, follow-on conduction of several

defense of Alaska exercises in warmer months to account for the diversity of Alaska's environment. Assure that exercises are funded by all services and components to include National Guard Bureau. Extend personalized invitations to train in Alaska to other active and reserve component units abroad including our NATO partners and Arctic allies.

2. As related to fulltime/full spectrum Domain Awareness operations: Permanently assign 11th Airborne Division, AKNGJS, USCG, and NAVNORTH liaison officers to NORAD/ALCOM JOC in order to maintain constant and consistent "whole of defense" concept Domain Awareness approach across all components and services in order to reduce response times during emergencies. This will require additional staff to be assigned to the NORAD/ALCOM JOC to resource 24/7 operations. The National Guard Bureau will be required to resource the AKNGJS for 24/7 operations as well. It is highly recommended that the State of Alaska resource and consider placing three (3) ASDF Soldiers on full time State Active-Duty orders in order to resource the AKNGJOC appropriately. This will involve developing and resourcing communications capabilities across all military forces in Alaska. Develop a means of communications from the forward edges of the State to integrated command centers statewide and integrate those systems in order to develop an overlapping Domain Awareness operational system that is relevant and capable.

3. Re-organize, re-assign, and re-align the AKARNG to form the 3rd Brigade of the 11th Airborne Division as the "round out" brigade, complete with enablers, in order to streamline efficiencies between USNORTHCOM, USINDOPACOM, and USARPAC.

4. Additionally, assign two Special Forces Operational Detachment Alpha (ODA) teams and one SOF liaison element (SOF-LE) to coach, teach, mentor, train and advise the Alaska Army National Guard and the Alaska State Defense Force. Alaska personnel could inevitably find themselves embedded with indigenous forces in denied or remote areas of the State in an event such as that of external threat adversary aggression or incursion into the US homeland via an Alaska avenue of approach or even during a time of natural disaster.

5. Increase Communications Capability across all military forces in Alaska. <u>This is an identified "gap" in nearly all US Arctic strategics written to date.</u> Develop a means of communications from the forward edge of the State's borders to integrated command centers statewide. The NORAD/ALCOM JOC would require equipment such that the newly assigned LNOs from the various components could communicate to ground units, sea going or river vessels, and aircraft to develop a multi-layered communication system at all levels to ensure command and control, communications, and Domain Awareness operational systems that are constantly operational.

Conclusion

At the outset of this chapter, the question was asked; "Are we prepared to meet adversarial threats to the US homeland specifically in Alaska?" The answer to this question is "no" as current preparations to defend the US homeland through an Alaska avenue of approach are either inadequate or worse, they are non-existent.

The problem of limited defense capabilities in Alaska is combined with the lack of overall preparedness through training and exercises specifically related to homeland defense. These problems are further compounded by the apparent confusion of leadership at the highest levels of multiple commands regarding just who is, or will be, in charge. This is a sentiment that is echoed in Lt. Col. Hoettels' article related to medical capability issues. Lt. Col. Hoettels writes:

"United States military medical support in the Arctic is further complicated by the fact responsibility for the defense of Alaska and the area north of the Arctic Circle is transregional, crossing three US geographic combatant command boundaries—US Northern Command, US Indo-Pacific Command, and US European Command. Yet a consensus on what organization is the lead for coordinating Arctic medical concepts and operations does not exist. Medical assets from these geographic combatant commands and service components work on individual capabilities and request funding separately for their respective projects."

As presented, there is a deficiency of effective communication across commands of just how US ground forces, and potentially other forces as well, in Alaska would be utilized if needed to defend the homeland. In conjunction, there is a next to non-existent "boots on the ground" domain awareness capability. The potential, and overall shortage of preparedness across the ground forces spectrum, in Alaska to accomplish the mission of being "masters" in Arctic war-fighting, as stated by General McConville, is tremendously hindered by the absence of an integrated operational "system" and a Joint Arctic Homeland Defense Strategy. As it currently stands, there exists no integrated focus among the services for a Joint Arctic Strategy.

As the world continues to focus on the Russian efforts in Ukraine, Putin and his Arctic ambitions continue to play out in a "long game" that began more than two decades ago. NATO is currently distracted by what is transpiring in Ukraine while the Russians (and most likely Chinese as well) continue to move forward with astounding progress in the Arctic. In 2022, Russian Foreign Minister Sergei Lavrov delivered the statement that Russia is at war with NATO. Although later rhetoric from the Foreign Minister was significantly toned down, Lavrov's statement, and the fact that Russian strategic aircraft continue to fly in the skies near Alaska, is no coincidence in timing. It is pure messaging.

The challenges and issues presented in this chapter should be addressed and remedied sooner rather than later. As the DNI stated in the threat assessment in 2022, the threat is real and so is the adversarial capability and intent. Alaska is a state that stands far removed from the flag poles and hallowed hallways of the Pentagon but a potential "Red Dawn" reality, as openly identified in the DNI threat assessment, is gravely different in the Last Frontier. The issues and challenges which have been presented in this chapter are ripe for foreign adversary exploitation in conjunction with tremendous risk and potential for US homeland incursion.

Chapter 8

Train As We Fight

In order to properly prepare for a potential invasion and/or occupation by adversary forces, AKOM members must train accordingly. Training for the sake of training in order to "check the box" of annual mandated training and briefings is simply inadequate for the real-world mission that AKOM members could easily face. Training for AKOM members should be directly reflective of the Arctic Strategy, the threat that will be faced (and is currently being presented), with training taking place in the actual environment where the hostilities might occur.

AKOM must re-focus its efforts by spending more time training and preparing for hostile events and resistance operations in the Arctic while dedicating the remainder of its time on domestic emergency preparation and response. As domestic emergencies arise, AKOM members can easily be re-tasked for the specific emergency for the period of duration however, the primary mission of AKOM should now be focused on deterrence and defense of Alaska.

Arctic Eagle 2022 Exercise: Invitation for Exercise Input

On 19 August 2020, a request for exercise input came in the form of a Memorandum of Invitation regarding Arctic Eagle 2022 Exercise Input from the Joint Staff Director, Alaska National Guard. The invitation "announces the exercise planning process and provides key guidance to plan, design, test, and execute ARCTIC EAGLE 2022." The memorandum sent forth included Exercise Objectives (EOs) and asked for the identification of areas of concern as related specifically to the EOs provided.

The areas of concern which were personally identified and submitted for exercise input on 11 September 2020 regarding the EOs of Arctic Eagle 2022 are listed below. It is suspected that the response personally submitted to this "invitation" was disregarded with justification of my suspicion being based on firsthand experiences in both Iraq and Afghanistan. It was repetitively demonstrated that high-ranking military members typically do not listen to civilian advisement on input where defense issues are concerned.

Areas identified and submitted on 11 September 2020, based on their established EO's were as follows:

1. EO 1: Generate Combat Readiness.
    - Is "Combat Readiness" actually generated by holding this exercise once every two years? Is the training cycle adequate to achieve "Combat Readiness" and if so, what is the standard utilized in measuring and accurately determining "Combat Readiness"?
    - How is "Combat Readiness" defined? Is "Combat Ready" determined to be defined as combat capable and combat effective for the Arctic environment of Alaska?
    - Does sending DOD personnel to other countries for Arctic Warfare training provide for combat ready, combat capable, and combat effective forces in the Arctic of Alaska? Why not train in the Arctic of Alaska where the fight will be? Training in Alaska provides for key terrain and cultural knowledge of the battlefield.
    - Is "projection" of combat power equivalent to combat readiness, capability, or combat effectiveness of US forces in Alaska when assessed by our adversaries? Are our forces actually combat ready, capable, and effective or are we "projecting" the illusion that they are?

2. EO 2: Identify Arctic Capability Gaps.
    - Inadequate defense capability to protect US assets from high altitude EMP detonation.[12]
    - Inadequate missile defense capability for response or intercept of container ship/submarine launched cruise missiles such as the Russian 3M-54 Kalibr (aka: The Club-

---

[12]This information was obtained in a recently published paper, *"Upgrading our Arctic Defenses,"* by Alaskan Ric Davidge. Additional information available as footnote in Chapter 2.

K)[13] which are now maintained by Russia, China, North Korea, and Iran.[14]

- If EMP detonation were to occur over selected targets of Anchorage, Nenana, and Kodiak, virtually all US defense capabilities (air, land, missile, communications, cyber, power, etc.) would be rendered inoperable in large, densely populated areas.

- If EMP detonation were to occur over selected targets, there would exist inadequate capability to protect coastal Early Warning Detection and National Weather Service radar sites with air assets or otherwise. Alaska and other Major Commands would be "blind" to follow-on activity of threat forces which would potentially allow for air superiority to be achieved over much of interior Alaska and coastal areas by foreign forces.

- Satellite coverage will be impacted by cloud coverage/inclement weather as is noted in DAF Arctic Defense Strategy 2020.[15]

- Inadequate DOD presence ("footprint") or access to many outlying areas, villages, or communities. This leads to "low density domain awareness" across the force as also identified in Air Force Arctic Defense Strategy.

- Excessive focus on areas of Anchorage, Fairbanks, and Juneau unless in emergency situations. Must get into the villages and communities for outreach and relationship building.[16]

---

[13] Information on 3M-54 Kalibr capabilities can be found at the *Wikipedia* page https://en.wikipedia.org/wiki/3M-54_Kalibr

[14] See footnote six from Chapter 2.

[15] The Department of the Air Force Arctic Strategy, July 2020.

[16] Alaska Department of Military and Veterans Affairs, Alaska National Guard. 2021-2024 Strategy. Adjutant General and Commissioner Intent. "*Our Operational Environment.*"

- Neglect to gain early access to the population in order to build trust with local leadership and the community.[17]
- Lack of implementation in the area of ground force multiplication process of "by/with/through" with the assistance of the local population. Forgotten lessons learned that "the center of gravity is the population" in any conflict. This has been stated in countless Field Manuals associated with counterinsurgency and stability operations. Alaska will be no different as operations will need to be prosecuted through UW methods via a majority civilian population resistance organization(s) in occupied areas.
- Need AKOM(ASDF) detachment development in key strategic areas implemented as an ISR and domain awareness asset in order to assist with timely and accurate information collection for inclusion into the comprehensive "living" IPB process.
- Need to assess strategic, operational, and tactical level advantages provided by ASDF and explore their roles and capabilities as aligned with DOD Arctic Strategy.
- Encourage "outside the box" thinking for innovation in a resource constrained environment.[18]
- Inadequate preparation of the "Alaska Battlefield" is due primarily to the continued limited knowledge and lack of understanding of the operational environment.

3. EO 3: Validate multi-modal transportation capabilities.
- Utilization of sled and freight dog teams for mobility through otherwise denied or typically impassable areas for troops and logistical supply. The US used this asset during WWII in the Aleutian Islands for these very purposes. ASDF maintains the capability to recruit these services from many communities where they live.

---

[17] Ibid.

[18] Alaska Department of Military and Veterans Affairs, Alaska National Guard. 2021-2024 Strategy. *"3. Innovate and Leverage,"* paragraph a.

- The Russians have been extensively utilizing sled-dog teams at the tactical level since WWII and have in recent years begun actively training forces in their employment.
- Snowmobile utilization is an approved form of military transportation in the Arctic environment and should be extensively utilized when possible.
- Consideration of enlisting/retaining Alaskan guides to provide alternative access (trails, passes, etc.) around/through denied or inaccessible areas.

4. EO 6: Conduction of multi-component and multi-national integration.
   - Lack of recognition of AKOM roles and capabilities as aligned with DOD Arctic Strategy and the integration of AKOM forces with other DOD components for combat operations and intelligence collection.
   - Lack of encouragement for AKOM strategic partnership with SOF for training in regard to force multiplication.

5. EO 7: Conduct domain awareness patrols.
   - Prior to conducting active patrols, identify key strategic areas for information collection and why they are such. How are these keys to the Arctic Strategy and defense of Alaska?
   - Collect open-source information on these areas by utilizing ASCOPE/PMESII matrix and SWEAT-MUS-R-O assessment in order to identify local and cultural knowledge gaps prior to conducting any patrols.
   - Develop an understanding that domain awareness includes more than geographical or physical features. Domain awareness is also inclusive of the population as well as their culture and cultural norms.
   - Develop an understanding of how the population fits into the context of the irregular warfare mission if necessary. This

reinforces the necessity of an AKOM strategic partnership with SOF.[19]

- Develop an understanding of how our adversaries implement and execute counterinsurgency strategy and operations.[20] Understand that these strategies and operations would be utilized against the Alaskan population if an insurgency or resistance were to arise.
- Develop an understanding of how the local population of a given area might respond to an invasion or occupation by foreign forces. Will they resist? Why or why not? Identify historical grievances of the population towards governance.
- Understand the history of the population and their relationship (if any) with foreign adversaries. Will they stay and oppose foreign forces, will they retreat to even more remote areas for the duration, or will they succumb to the rule of the occupiers? This can be discovered through cultural knowledge capture.
- Send small teams (3-4 personnel) into these areas to establish contact with local leadership (formal and informal) for relationship building and area evaluation. Create opportunities now for Key Leader Engagements.
- Do not overwhelm the village or community being assessed with a large group. Local perceptions are vital. Keep military "footprint" small.

---

[19] Army Field Manual 3-05.130, *Army Special Operations Forces Unconventional Warfare*, pages 1-4 through 1-8, describes the effectiveness and implementation of the population in the Irregular Warfare context as applied to conventional military operations. It is about the people.

[20] The Russians learned their lessons in counterinsurgency in the most difficult manner in Afghanistan yet, they failed to learn many historical lessons learned there. The Russians implemented brutal, but effective, counterinsurgency tactics in Chechnya with a "heavy handed" approach (known as the Authoritarian Model). This resulted in the quelling or elimination of the Chechnyan insurgency as is reported in Small Wars Journal. Though the Russian forces met with significant issues and difficulties in Chechnya, this author presents that Russian counterinsurgency efforts were significantly more successful there than compared to US efforts in Afghanistan. Source from: https://smallwarsjournal.com/jrnl/art/the-other-side-of-the-coin-the-russians-in-chechnya

- Personnel must be cognizant of cultural norms in remote/semi-remote communities. Smart, personable people are necessary for this mission. Not strictly outsiders of Alaska.
- Do not conduct domain awareness patrols in unlikely areas just for the sake of exercise purposes. Make this a "real world" portion of the exercise. Begin building relationships while gathering critical information. Contact key leadership of communities in advance for permission to visit prior to the arrival of forces.
- Integrate AKOM (ASDF) personnel with other component force personnel for this mission. AKOM personnel live in Alaska, and they are the base of cultural knowledge for other component forces. Allow AKOM to Lead, Liaise, Advise, and Assist (L2A2) other component forces in this regard.
- Utilize Key Leader Engagements in villages and communities to "grow the force" for future needs. AKOM members must be the "Ambassadors."

6. EO 8: Support the National Guard Arctic Interest Council (NG-AIC) Exercise Strategy
    - Where does one find the NG-AIC Exercise Strategy for review and comparison to current exercise planning of Arctic Eagle 2022?
    - How does one contact the NG-AIC direct for questions related to any of the aforementioned information pertaining to Exercise Objectives in 1-5 above?

In providing the information above, areas of concern of overall defense and military readiness in Alaska were identified. All information presented was obtained through unclassified, open-source collection methodology and has identified vulnerability and capability gaps as requested by the Director in his memorandum. Yet apparently, he chose to ignore the very "input" he had requested.

It should be asked and considered, what must our adversaries have readily identified in their assessments of defense and military capability in the Alaska area of operations? The answer of combat readiness, combat capability, and combat effectiveness of US forces in Alaska has been established as minimal and must be critically examined and defined as either ready, or simply presenting with the illusion as ready. This is where National and State Defense planning and preparation, as related specifically to Alaska and the Arctic Region, should have focused efforts.

Part II

Chapter 9

Understanding the Human Terrain

This chapter will directly support EO's 2, 3, and 7, from the previous chapter as related to the population and resistance operations should they become necessary in Alaska.

It would be wise for Commanders stationed in Alaska, as well as Commanders of units and teams who might find themselves operating anywhere in Alaska, to invest both time and money on training that promotes a firm comprehension of the human terrain of specific locations. In Alaska alone, there are numerous resources available which can provide volumes of information about the people in remote areas, their history, and their culture. It is contended that this is also the case for every other Arctic Nation and their populations as well given that research has revealed as much.

To the contrary however, it often seems that the vast number of resources available actually contribute to the problem of undermining the process of gaining an in-depth knowledge and comprehension of the human terrain and their associated cultures in a given battlespace. Far too many strategists choose to "ask the internet" for broad based, and particular, information instead of asking someone from the culture for firsthand knowledge. One really needs to look no further than the difficulties encountered in both Iraq and Afghanistan for countless examples to reinforce this supposition.

It has been my experience that whenever many (but not all) military leaders have taken the time to read a book or two on the subject matter of another ethnicity and their culture, these leaders tend to believe that they have become cultural experts overnight. In actuality, what they have done is foment the problem which generates even more confusion for themselves and worse, for those in their charge. Several military and civilian leaders I have worked with have chosen to "go with what they know" instead of actively seeking to expand their knowledge from a trusted cultural advisor.

From July 2009 through November 2010, I was assigned to a Human Terrain Team (HTT) in Logar and Wardak Provinces of Afghanistan. During my time in country, our HTT was attached to 3/10th Mountain, the 173rd

Airborne IBCT, and then 4/10th Mountain. At one time, there were approximately 15 HTT's spread across Afghanistan (and probably that many simultaneously in Iraq) and it is my belief that every team did outstanding work for the Army, the Marines, and even some NATO allies to which they were attached. Yet, what was to come was a vast number of articles written about the HTS project that highlighted all of its failures.

Without a doubt, the program certainly had its share of failures however, there also existed an exorbitant amount of successes. What has seldom been written about are those successes which were created by the teams "downrange" and the members who actively took part in what would become a highly criticized Department of the Army special project. Through all of the spears and arrows hurled in their direction, compounded by suspicion and doubt, the large percentage of HTS members remained focused on their tasks and succeeded in the face of near impossibility with little, and often at times no, support.

The very premise of the project was to embed CIV/MIL teams with deployed units in order to provide Commanders with *operationally relevant information* specific to the understanding of the local population and their culture (i.e., the human terrain). The information provided was based on culture (and all that might entail) as well as the potential 1st, 2nd, and 3rd order effects, as perceived by the local population, caused by both friendly and adversary force actions or operations. The concept was exceptionally solid and highly advantageous for those Commanders who were not risk averse to absorbing the HTT's information and saw the benefit of their gainful employment.

A Human Terrain Team member meets with Pashtun tribal elders in Afghanistan. Retrieved from: https://www.wired.com/2008/04/gates-human-ter/

A significant advantage that the HTT's provided was the fact that a team did not "rotate out" with a departing unit. Instead, the team remained in place and overlapped indefinitely. This equated to a tremendous amount of information and knowledge being captured and shared with incoming units. HTT's often had people on the ground who already maintained knowledge of the battlespace and associations with many "key leaders" due to members (or the Team) having already been in the location for an extended period of time. There was no "reinvention of the wheel" (so to speak) for incoming units and Commanders, it was sheer continuity.

Though the concept of the project was sound as stated, the HTS project unfortunately ended due to reasons which simply could not be overcome. By the time new management arrived in the form of Colonel Sharon Hamilton, the damage was too far gone to be undone. COL Hamilton did her best, and made some outstanding changes, yet she simply could not move HTS out of the overshadowing perceptions of many critics of the project who sat comfortably on committees in the Politico-Military arena. Critics who were, by that time, inclusive of many who had sung the praises of HTS in years prior.

While some may attempt to argue otherwise, the HTS project was pure Cultural Intelligence (CULINT) and Ethnographic Intelligence (ETHINT) at its very core. In conjunction with this was the fact that this project fell directly under the Training and Doctrine Command (TRADOC) Intelligence Support Activity-G2. This fact has always been a point of contention for many social scientists that were part of the HTS project, and even more of those who were not. But the "muddy waters" created by individual, or collective, Social Scientist perception does not in any way change what the project was in reality.

The HTS project assisted the COIN effort through the deployment of numerous teams specializing in cultural matters in both Afghanistan and Iraq. In hindsight, this project could very easily have collected and produced invaluable information in conflicts now existing all over the globe, potentially changing many undesired outcomes on a large scale. A program such as this still maintains its value and should be provided with a second chance. Honestly and personally speaking, the Arctic Region (in this case Alaska) is an excellent place to provide the opportunity.

In stating all of this about HTS, there is a valid point and/or argument to be made. With the Department of the Army recognizing the need for a program such as this to be utilized in both Iraq and Afghanistan (and Africa to some extent) to assist with operationally relevant, cultural information for Commanders in those locations, then it should stand to logically conclude that a similar type of program is warranted for utilization in the Arctic Region. This is supported by the fact that so many different ethnicities and cultures also exist in the region. Why would the entire Department of Defense exclude such an operationally relevant consideration from all of their Arctic strategies when it has been proven to be a _highly effective_ UW methodology?

It is recommended that Commanders take the initiative and seek innovative ways to create their own HTT's and begin utilizing them appropriately. All of the information that should be researched and obtained relating to culture is unclassified and available through numerous resources including the internet. Understanding the human terrain has been proven to be one of the most critical aspects of current warfighting methodology during both the 20th and 21st centuries and it is incomprehensible that every lesson learned, in the last 22 years alone specifically related to this subject, would be omitted from inclusion in Arctic Strategy. If future conflict arises anywhere in the Arctic Region and US troops are deployed, then every advantage must be afforded to them. One of the advantages of utmost importance is providing them with information in order to understand the human terrain in an area of operations.

Forging Relationships with the Population

AKOM elements have access to the population in many remote communities where other DOD forces do not. As stated, many AKOM members reside in some of these communities where assistance to US forces (particularly SOF) will be necessary.

An article dated 27 April 2021 states that the Army is seeking help from all over the world in order to regain "dominance" in the Arctic Region. Army Major General Peter Andrysiak, former Commander of US Army Alaska, was even quoted as saying, "What we're trying to do as we move forward with this is expand our relationships with other allies and partners that have to operate in a similar environment," (where he specifically mentions Norway, Finland,

and Sweden). MG Andrysiak is further quoted as saying, "We've been given the green light to ... start working with other allies and partners, and that includes Norway and the other allies and partners up in that area," and 'We know that there's a lot that we have to learn, because obviously Norway has a great history of being able to operate in and through that particular environment.'

What is absent from this approach in the Army's own strategy is the need to "Consider the knowledge of Indigenous populations to improve Arctic expertise" as is identified on p. 36 of the published US Army Arctic Strategy in 2021. It is stated in this section that:

"Indigenous populations, the myriad autonomous societies, have thrived in Alaska and Arctic territory for millennia. They know the environment, wildlife, and terrain better than anyone. Learning this information from them will be valuable in understanding how to not only survive, but to train and thrive in the Arctic and in other extreme cold-weather, and mountainous environments. The Army will consider this knowledge and expertise to improve individual and unit training for Arctic capable formations."

If the Army has identified this consideration as being of such importance in its own Arctic Strategy, then it is strongly believed that obtaining knowledge from those living within the operational environment of Alaska would be of primary importance and the Army would seek-out that knowledge. Instead, the Army is approaching the situation by first seeking out information globally instead of locally. This approach demonstrates immediate divergence from its very own strategy and outwardly presents with an absence of logic.

While it is important to seek knowledge associated with operating militarily in a foreign Arctic environment from other nations, it is of equal, if not greater, importance to understand the operational environment where US Arctic forces are currently positioned and could very well find themselves in conflict. In accordance with the Army Arctic Strategy, the understanding and knowledge of operating in America's Arctic should come directly from the Indigenous population of Alaska, not from the military partners of Norway, Finland, or Sweden.

Chapter 10

Relationships with Irregulars

There have likely been countless scenarios and wargames conducted concerning the Arctic Region and Alaska by NORAD and NORTHCOM. As well, Special Operations Command North (SOCNORTH) has probably also conducted wargaming exercises concerning the region in accordance with the National Defense Strategy as was also complimented by the 2019 DOD Arctic Strategy and the USAF Arctic Strategy of 2020. Yet what seems to be consistently absent is the consideration and utilization of the local population in the event of an invasion or occupation of Alaska. Additionally, the value a prepared population can provide in the context of the overall strategy has perhaps also been absent in scenario consideration.

Questions should be asked regarding the military considerations given in each of the strategies and wargame exercises conducted. Questions such as:

> 1. Have there been considerations taken in these scenarios of the 2nd and 3rd order effects of military operations on the population in these potentially denied areas of operations (MDMP)?[21]

> 2. Have there been considerations taken as to how a small, capable detachment of the AKOM personnel located in a denied community might be utilized in the overall effort against an invasion or occupation?

> 3. Have there been considerations given as to how strategically located detachments of AKOM personnel might be utilized in leading local efforts for guerrilla warfare or resistance operations against the occupiers in these areas?

> 4. Have there been considerations given as to how the population of occupied areas, which have been organized and prepared as a

---

[21] Center for Army Lessons Learned. Handbook No.15-06, *"MDMP Lessons and Best Practices."* March 2015.

resistance force well in advance, might assist in their geographical locations?

The answers to these questions are currently unknown however, computers and leadership often neglect to factor in friendly irregular forces or the local population and their capabilities. This mindset must change and along with it, changes to existing strategies must be implemented.

There are several irregular/unorganized militia groups within Alaska. While some of these groups are often labeled as radical elements with a skewed vision of Constitutional defense (which some may have), others are often inappropriately profiled as being radical as well. All may speak openly against Constitutional infringement and outwardly pose as the defenders of the Second Amendment yet, labeling every irregular/unorganized militia group and its members as radical is equivalent to mislabeling all Trump supporters as deplorables or insurrectionists. While this section will be adamantly contested by some in both military and political circles, we should consider some historical facts prior to dismissing altogether the concept of actively working with irregular forces.

The facts for consideration are those associated with whom the US has historically allied itself with in Afghanistan and those we continuously turned a "blind-eye" towards based on the premise of who is the lesser of evils. For example, did we not ally ourselves with some less than desirable people and organizations in order to advance policy and strategic objectives long before the US invaded Afghanistan in 2001? The answer is absolutely yes, and we did it favorably and frequently during the Soviet-Afghan War in the 1980's. In fact, one of the most prominent Afghan fighters that we supported during that conflict was Jalaluddin Haqqani who, as described by Steve Coll in his book *Ghost Wars,* was a "less publicized CIA favorite" in addition to having "had the CIA's full support." When the US invaded Afghanistan in late 2001 however, the Haqqani Network had switched their allegiance to the Taliban and would go on to harass US and NATO efforts for many years until the complete US and NATO withdrawal in August 2021.

During time spent in (and associated with) Afghanistan, many interesting things transpired. There was the conceptualization and attempted institution of an internationally supported "Reconciliation and Reintegration Program" that was specifically aimed at influencing the Taliban to no longer fight against

NATO and ISAF forces with guarantees of their peaceful reintegration into society. Simply lay down your arms, sign an agreement, attend some classes, and we will find you a new home. Yes, that is how it was supposed to work. It was a modern-day version of the Chieu Hoi program from Vietnam, and it is a prime example of McNamara's previously quoted statement about the lack of knowledge of the people and their culture. The human terrain of Afghanistan was absolutely *"terra incognita."*

We frequently switched sides ourselves in Afghanistan. We supported Gulbuddin Hekmatyar, whose organization Hezb-i-Islami-Gulbuddin (HIG, a faction we also supported during the Soviet-Afghan war), was once in the top five on the list of insurgent networks we were actively targeting in Afghanistan along *with* the Haqqani Network. And then there is General Abdul Rashid Dostum who initially began as an ally to the US immediately following 9/11 however, Dostum switched sides too, at some point, opposing us (albeit indirectly). But then Dostum switched sides again and went on to become the Vice President of Afghanistan from September 2014 until February 2020. This was all with the full support of the US and NATO. Are you scratching or shaking your head yet?

We should consider what we have done in Afghanistan (and other places) and the people and organizations we supported long before we pass any type of judgment and neglect to establish relationships with American irregular forces in the American Arctic. In considering whom all we have conducted business with to achieve US Policy and Strategic objectives abroad, outright dismissal of building relationships with *some* US irregulars in Alaska due to loosely based perspectives would be hypocritical. Extremely hypocritical given our historically questionable and unethical relationships developed with others elsewhere around the globe (i.e., Iran-Contra).

In accordance with Alaska Statute 26.05.10, all "able-bodied persons" over the age of 17 meeting eligibility requirements and who reside in the state, not serving in the organized militia, are subject to service if called upon by the Governor. In the event of invasion or occupation by foreign forces, we in no way should believe that any members of irregular/unorganized militia groups would be turned away from serving during a time of National Defense. To the contrary, we would seek their assistance in denied or occupied areas if for no reasons other than their knowledge of the area, for intelligence collection, for access to their networks, and for assistance with resistance operations.

In contemplation of the information provided, it is believed that official relationships should be formalized with *some* of these groups long before their service might be required. Arctic Strategy should consist of regular planning with these groups "in the event of..." so that there is a mutual understanding of what role the irregular forces will assume if needed and an understanding of how they will assist in overall resistance strategy and operations.

Once a relationship is established with irregulars, joint training with military elements should occur as frequently as possible. Security Force Assistance and SOF personnel, working in tandem with ASDF members, would be ideal in providing this training to irregulars. Doing so would cultivate the relationships by continuing to build trust between the organized and irregular forces, serve to establish relationships between chains of command, provide for unity of effort (State, Local, Federal and population,), and prevent redundancy of effort (due to misunderstandings or lack of guidance) in future operations when the irregulars are called upon to assist.

Accessing the Population and Force Multiplication

In the overall framework of DOD Arctic Strategy, it has been discussed that the population is frequently overlooked as related to the Homeland Defense portion of the strategy. As stated, AKOM has access to the population of many remote communities of Alaska where other active component DOD entities do not. Many AKOM members reside in remote communities where word of mouth and trust are the greatest recruiting tools and where assistance to US forces will be necessary. This is all being discussed again because the importance of this fact cannot be overly stated.

The critical aspect of access to remote populations is far beyond the current scope and practice of many DOD entities or organizations in Alaska. This shortcoming is due primarily to self-imposed restrictions and limitations on the areas of Anchorage, Juneau, and Fairbanks. These major operational hubs present in much the same manner as did larger Forward Operating Bases (FOBs) in Iraq and Afghanistan and as a common "side-effect," most attention was paid to the immediate areas surrounding the FOBs. This fact hindered US efforts for years in enlisting the trust and services of the population across both countries. With the given circumstances, the current approach to Homeland Defense related to Arctic Strategy appears that restriction to the areas around the primary Alaskan operational hubs is now presenting in the same manner and yielding similar "side-effects" as did those in Iraq and Afghanistan.

If the desire exists for the population of Alaska to come to the aid of US defense in the Arctic via resistance means, with respect to the Homeland Defense of our Nation and our State, then the population must be approached with the commitment to build relationships, establish trust with the community, and keep promises made. Times have changed since the inception of the Alaska Territorial Guard and a willingness to fight. The population at large in Alaska routinely exhibits fluctuational trust in governance and even less trust in government leadership. No longer can it be assumed that our government, or its representatives, have the presence or respect to appeal to the patriotism of the populace. Heart-felt appeals espousing patriotism may not be sufficient to enlist the needed assistance of the population thereby, the appeals for assistance will fall on "deaf ears" or "cold shoulders." This assertion is based on the historical actions, and inactions, of governance exhibited over the past decades.

Early and repeated access to remote villages and communities, and their population and leadership, is a key component in relationship building within those communities. This approach goes hand-in-hand with regard to establishing a potentially necessary resistance movement *prior* to an occupation event. Again, this would be effective force implementation for force multiplication and is a potential strength for further AKOM integration into Arctic Strategy.

If our two decades long involvement in counterinsurgency efforts in both Iraq and Afghanistan has taught us anything, it is that we know that the people are the center of gravity in any area of conflict. This has already been stated. Inasmuch, why should such a valuable lesson learned abroad be so willingly neglected when it can be readily applied to the concept of Homeland Defense in Alaska? To strongly support this point, it is documented in a RAND publication written by author Charles T. Cleveland, *"The American War of Irregular War: An Analytical Memoir,"* that:

"American irregular warfare is the United States' unique, and in recent times troubled, approach to conflict in which armed civilian or paramilitary forces, and not regular armies, are the primary combatants. In most forms, it emphasizes the importance of local partnerships and gaining legitimacy and influence among targeted populations. It is thus a critical capability in contests where populations, rather than territory, are decisive."

Waiting until a population becomes denied or difficult to access during an occupation is a strategic failure, at the most fundamental level, and this failure will cost lives during attempts to access it after the fact. Gaining early access to the population, building relationships and trust with the leadership and population of these areas during peacetime, in concomitance with developing small detachments of AKOM personnel in these areas, should be immediate objectives of AKOM. Doing so will correspond directly with the Arctic Strategy.

Chapter 11

Culture

Culture, as defined by Merriam-Webster online, is:

"The customary beliefs, social forms, and material traits of a racial, religious, or social group, also, the characteristic features of everyday existence (such as diversions or a way of life) shared by people in a place or time."

We can also define culture by exploring the Social Science fields of anthropology, ethnology, and sociology for their definitions whereby our exploration reveals to us the definitions provided by the website www.thefreedictionary.com. Anthropology and Ethnology defines culture as:

"The total range of activities and ideas of a group of people with shared traditions, which are transmitted and reinforced by members of the group."
The same website has Sociology defining culture as *"the total of the inherited ideas, beliefs, values, and knowledge, which constitute the shared bases of social action."*

As exhibited by the definitions provided, defining culture can be a bit confusing and is varied, even debated, even across academia. For the purpose of this chapter, it is believed that the best definition of culture is provided in FM 3-24, Chapter 3, section 3-3 where it is stated that:

"Culture is a web of meaning shared by members of a particular society or group within a society."

The most important part of the definition provided by FM 3-24 is the recognition that culture is a web of *"meaning shared by members"* of a society. If we loosely translate *meaning* to become *beliefs*, we see that it becomes a web of *beliefs* shared by members of a society. To be more tangible, it is a system of beliefs shared amongst members of a particular group or groups. It is, therefore, no wonder that like-minded people tend to gravitate towards one another which, in turn, indicates that a culture of common beliefs already pre-existed and will strengthen over time.

Understanding the importance of culture in the Alaskan Arctic COE is advantageous to US forces that will be operating there, and it is a critical component of Arctic Strategy that is minimized. US forces operating in the Arctic must maintain prior knowledge and understanding of the Indigenous cultures in their area of operations prior to their arrival in order to enhance, or initiate, Arctic Homeland Defense capability. If approaching the Indigenous population for knowledge and support specifically for resistance operations is a recognized part of the Army Arctic Strategy, then the Army <u>must</u> value the importance of establishing relationships and obtaining cultural knowledge of the Indigenous population *prior* to its actual entry into a battlespace. Again, a valuable lesson learned from both Afghanistan and Iraq, but one that is being neglected.

In referring back to an abundance of information previously discussed, understanding the human terrain, the various cultures, and the cultural norms are three absolutely essential elements in engaging with the population in order to build rapport and establish trust. A fourth, and often typically unthought of, essential element is that of history. Not just past or present, but also future. This is especially important when engaging with cultures of Native tribes however, these four critically essential elements are applicable in all locations where Native populations are found, no matter how urban or remote.

In his book, *"Tribal Engagement: History, Law, and War as Operational Elements,"* author and former US Army Special Forces Officer Patrick James Christian depicts the often-overlooked importance of the element of history while simultaneously, and indirectly, stressing the importance of effective listening. Christian states that:

"The historical narrative of any tribe or cultural-political entity is an imaginative story that describes in near mythical detail the origins of the tribe, its growth, triumphs, defeats and struggles with redemption and salvation. Where history is a collection of events in chronological order, historical narrative provides the tribe with meaning of those events, forming a basis for collective memory and group identity."

During many key leader engagements which I took part of in Afghanistan, Afghan leaders (often elders or Mullahs) would speak metaphorically about subjects such as current local conditions, tribal history, or the history of the area itself. If a military or civilian member of the engagement team was not an effective listener, as was often the case, they would miss the true meaning of what they were being told. This lack of cultural understanding typically resulted in the US members frequently walking away from the engagement scratching their heads in frustration. This witnessed fact illustrated that there was a breakdown in the most fundamental understanding of the culture and cultural norms of the Afghan population and there existed the overt absence of prior cultural knowledge. The example provided from Afghanistan now exemplifies the need for advanced development of effective listening skills on the part of those who will be engaging with key formal and informal leaders of remote Arctic villages or communities and the importance of maintaining the well-educated ability to clearly "send and receive" messages cross-culturally.

As was also learned in both Afghanistan and Iraq, not everything is easily translatable cross-culturally. A localized example of this in the American Arctic, and one that also reinforces Mr. Christian's statement about history, is provided by Ms. Clare Swan in the book, *"Alaska Native Cultures and Issues: Responses to frequently asked questions."* Ms. Swan, a member of the Dena'ina tribe of Alaska, states:

"For far too long, we Dena'ina people have been trying to tell our story in other people's words. This may explain some of why we've been almost invisible in our own country, even among ourselves."

In examining Ms. Swan's statement more in-depth, she provides us with a glimpse of how the process of assimilation has been imposed on the Dena'ina tribe. Hidden within the process, has been the expectation that their tribal story, or their history more accurately, should be told in the words of others and not that of their own. This demonstrates the theft of their tribal cultural identity to the point of being "almost invisible."

As Ms. Swan's statement demonstrates, much is lost in translation. Instead of seeking the knowledge required to understand what others of different cultures are attempting to tell us in their own words, it has become an acceptable practice to replace their words with our own. In doing so, as has been the case in Iraq, Afghanistan, and now Alaska, it causes us to miss the message entirely. The end result being that we often make un-recoverable errors due to cultural bias.

Cultural and Ethnographic Information

Benjamin T. Delp stated the importance of maintaining cultural and ethnographic information prior to entering any conflict. Mr. Delp stated that, "While high ranking military officers and commanders on the ground have only recently begun to recognize the importance of ethnographic and cultural intelligence for success in Iraq, decision-makers in Washington, D.C. must understand the value of analyzing foreign populations' cultural identities prior to, during, and after US military intervention for current US objectives to be realized."[22] Mr. Delp's statement is insightfully accurate and also highly applicable to the tribes inhabiting the American Arctic.

Stake holding Commands such as NORAD, USNORTHCOM, ALCOM, USINDOPACOM, USINDOPACOM, SOCNORTH, and AKOM should underline the importance of this subject. Strides should be taken for program development specifically designed to "capture" cultural and ethnographic information and knowledge related to the American Arctic and its inhabitants, how this information can be applied to enhancing Homeland Defense and future Arctic operations, and how this information will assist the warfighting capability of forces supporting resistance operations.

Cultural and ethnographic information is an integral part of strategy and planning when applied to the CCOE component of the IPB process. Caution is advised in utilizing the word "intelligence" and should be replaced with "information." This is due to the fact that data being collected on friendly populations could be misconstrued as that of a form of a "Big Brother" concept. Vast amounts of cultural information are readily available via open-source research as well as through institutions such as the Alaska Federation

---

[22] Benjamin T. Delp is the Director of Research Development and Promotion at James Madison University. He is also the author of the 2008 paper, "Ethnographic Intelligence (ETHINT) and Cultural Intelligence (CULINT): Employing under-utilized strategic intelligence gathering disciplines for more effective diplomatic and military planning."

of Natives, the University of Alaska, and comparable sites or organizations of other nations.

The Cultural Advisor

According to FM 3-24, *"Counterinsurgency,"* Chapter 3, section 3-20, states that cultural advisors are personnel who are a part of a concept developed during Operation Enduring Freedom in Afghanistan. The manual specifically states:

"Cultural advisors are the principal subject matter experts on culture and planning related to their designated geographic region of expertise, serving as the cultural and language advisors to the commander. The cultural advisor is a special staff officer for the commander and a member of the planning staff. This person not only serves on the planning staff, but also deploys and serves as an ongoing advisor to senior leaders while they are in theater, if needed. The advantage of having a cultural advisor on staff is that this advisor can often help explain to the commander what the advisor sees on the ground in the area of operations. A foreign area officer or a civil affairs Soldier may be a good selection for a cultural advisor. Both can provide an understanding of the host nation and its specific regional, religious, and ethnic differences, and they may have foreign language skills. As a result, the commander can adjust operations in response to a culturally challenging environment."

It is agreed with what FM 3-24 has stated however, there are certain aspects which are disagreed with. First, the cultural advisor should not be a special staff officer or even a military member. Second, neither a Foreign Area Officer nor a Civil Affairs Soldier are good selections for cultural advisors. While any of these people could serve in a short-term capacity, none should maintain the position for any long-term period unless there is no other option.

The best cultural advisors will be found only through utilizing the very guidance set forth in the first sentence as presented above:

"Cultural advisors are the principal subject matter experts on culture and planning related to their designated geographic region of expertise, serving as the cultural and language advisors to the commander."

Simply stated, the best cultural advisor to a Commander (or team) pertaining to a designated geographical region is a person *from* the local culture. These are the people who should be sought out and employed by US forces. If at all possible, employ those who grew up within the culture and speak the Native language, not someone who has merely studied the culture and speaks none (or extraordinarily little) of the language, potentially in an incorrect dialect.

It cannot be overstated that we must seek out knowledge from within the culture prior to needing it. This should be included in current training and preparation involved with Arctic Strategy and resistance operations.

Understanding Adversary Culture

Solely understanding adversarial military capability and intent is no longer sufficient for warfare in the modern age. In order to fully understand our adversary, we must seek knowledge about them from cultural resources that openly contribute information as to who they are as a people and what motivates them.

To reinforce the importance of the preceding paragraph, FM 3-0, *"Operations,"* is inclusive of a quote at the outset of the section on *"War and Warfare"* in Chapter 1. The included quote was written by two-time Pulitzer Prize recipient Barbara W. Tuchman and reads:

"We now need another voice of wisdom to tell us, "Technology is not enough." War is not one big engineering project. There are people on the other side— with strengths and will that we never bothered to measure. As a result of that omission, we have been drawn into a greater, and certainly more ruinous, belligerent action than we intended. To fight without understanding the opponent ultimately serves neither the repute of the military nor the repute of the nation."

The appearance of a quote such as this in a Department of the Army Field Manual is indicative of its exceptional importance and should not be omitted from integration into strategy. The quote strongly declares the consequences of neglecting to understand the adversary, their culture, and their beliefs. It further declares that doing so is an error in judgement by leadership that will result in ruin/failure.

In 2005, Dr. Montgomery McFate, a professor at the US Naval War College, authored the paper, *"Does Culture Matter? The Military Utility of Understanding Adversary Culture."* In her paper, Dr. McFate states:

"Cultural knowledge and warfare are inextricably bound. Cultural knowledge as a means to improve military prowess has been sought after since Herodotus concerned himself with the opponents' conduct during the Persian Wars (490 - 479 B.C.). T.E. Lawrence embarked on a similar quest for adversary knowledge after the 1916 Arab rebellion against the Ottoman Empire, immersing himself deeply in local culture: 'Geography, tribal structure, religion, social customs, language, appetites, standards were at my finger-ends. The enemy I knew almost like my own side. I risked myself among them many times, to learn.'"[23]

There is an abundance of readily available information about adversary cultures which could, in turn, provide us with significant insight into their military cultures and military mindsets. In what could be described as echoing Ms. Tuchman's previous quote, Dr. McFate further states that:

"...understanding one's enemy requires more than a satellite photo of an arms dump. Rather, it requires an understanding of their interests, habits, intentions, beliefs, social organizations, political symbols – in other words, their culture."

We often base our knowledge of our adversary strictly on their military capabilities and in doing so, we only collect a small fraction of information about them. As Mrs. Tuchman stated in relation to understanding our opponent, "Technology is not enough." This is yet another information "gap" that US Arctic Strategy is content with maintaining (though it is not definitively reported as such in any strategy). This information gap should be filled with cultural information and applied to our adversaries and their leadership in order to provide a more comprehensive picture of who is opposing us and what is motivating them to do so. This is information that Commanders can utilize to their advantage in much the same manner that some

---

[23] T.E. Lawrence as quoted in B.H. Liddell Hart, Lawrence of Arabia, p. 399. New York: DeCapo, 1989.

began to succeed with in both Iraq and Afghanistan. However, in both locations, this recognition and the associated successes came too late.

In order to firmly grasp an understanding of the human terrain in the Arctic during conflict, it is essential to also include an understanding of the culture of the enemy that could occupy that terrain as well. In only maintaining an understanding of adversarial war-fighting capability, enormous potential exists for underestimating the actions of the enemy. This perspective again lends itself to the value of maintaining knowledge of adversary cultures. In order to obtain a more significant understanding of our enemies, we must follow the advisement of Sun-Tzu:

"To know your enemy, you must become your enemy."

It must be stated that in order to think like our enemy, we must get past the superficiality of their known war-fighting capability associated with technology *and* the stereotypes of their culture. As has been well presented in US strategy, technology will fail in the Arctic and with technological failure so also goes many means of war-fighting capability of the adversary. In the same regard, what we think we might know about our enemy, as related to their culture, is based on decades of stereotyping which is an inaccurate assessment which will aid in producing further failure in the Arctic.

Questions that might be visited on the topic of understanding adversary culture will be vast, but typically pointed. Questions such as, what is their leadership most likely to do in a given situation and why? Or what might we discern about their leadership and that person's military mindset based on a cultural analysis of that person? Can a predictive analysis related to a particular situation produce desired 1st, 2nd, and 3rd order effects (leveraged effects) based on cultural knowledge considerations of our adversary? We applied this methodology to our adversaries in both Iraq and Afghanistan, so I see no reason why we should not apply it to our adversaries in the Arctic as well.

We can also apply Maslow's Hierarchy of Needs to the subject of adversary culture. In doing so, it should become clear that within the military culture of our adversary, all five levels of Maslow's Hierarchy are in play. When comparing this to the resistance and/or guerrilla culture, we see that the bottom three levels are those *primarily* applicable. The fourth level of "Esteem" will *become* applicable once freedom is obtained and with this, respect, status, recognition, and strength will follow.

As stated, there are countless resources available on the culture and history of our adversaries. It is strongly recommended that many of these resources be tapped and intensively studied by US forces long before entering into direct conflict with our near-peer adversaries.

Chapter 12

Changing Perceptions

Much has been written in numerous books, manuals, and articles about the importance of culture in the COE. For nearly two decades, sub-par, hurried training was inclusive of regional and area specific cultural awareness, cultural sensitivity, cultural traditions and norms, and cross-cultural communications associated with the Iraq and Afghanistan areas of operation. Some US personnel approached the training open-mindedly with positive attitudes which allowed them to develop and enhance their skillsets. This open-minded approach by a small portion of service members often provided them with a better understanding of their operational environment which in turn allowed for their tours of duty to be more successful.

However, there is an often-underreported and vastly differing perspective that provides for a high-quality "snapshot" that exposed that a large majority of military personnel adamantly resisted everything associated with the "soft skills" training. Cultural awareness and sensitivity simply were not war-fighting tools that American Soldiers, Sailors, Airmen, and Marines (outside of SOF or Advisory teams), were accustomed to applying. This sudden change in war-fighting infringed upon the "comfort zones" of the traditional military mind-set as related to their disciplines. This was counter-productive in many ways as the "close with and destroy" mentality was literally replaced overnight with "winning hearts and minds." Service members were being expected to "be nice" to everyone, even in known hostile operational environments. This approach was expected even after being engaged with roadside bombs, ambushes, or sniper fire received on the way to a nearby "friendly" village which military members would frequently visit. The forced change directly undermined the indoctrinated military mindset with the unintended consequences impacting operational effectiveness and the American military culture.

In 2004 or early 2005, some old jargon began making its way through the services. Leading the way in that military-lingo resurrection was the term "counterinsurgency." For those who retained knowledge of US military history, it appeared that some in the Pentagon, along with certain

Commander's in the Field, had dusted off a couple of old Vietnam era Field Manuals. Specifically, it appeared that Army FM 31-22, *"US Army Counterinsurgency Forces"* (published in November 1963) and Army FM 31-16, *"Counterguerrilla Operations"* (published in February 1963) were resources utilized by many. Eventually, Generals David Petraeus and John F. Amos headed the effort in constructing Army FM 3-24, *"Counterinsurgency,"* published in 2006. FM 3-24 would go on to become the very foundation for several additional FMs that followed written on the subject of COIN. It was the "Bible" for many concepts found in the supplementary manuals produced which were applied, and more often inappropriately applied, in both Iraq and Afghanistan.

There were consistent topics which appeared in many of the newly published COIN manuals. Two of the most common topics stressed the importance of culture and cultural knowledge of the population along with recognition of the fact that the population is the center of gravity in any conflict. These topics, as have been previously recognized for operations abroad, are now also incredibly important to Arctic Homeland Defense and potential RO in Alaska. This statement is based on the fact that Alaska is comprised of numerous Native tribes with differing cultures in conjunction with the fact that their assistance will be absolutely necessary as an integral part of defending the homeland in the US Arctic.

While it should be a bit of a "no brainer" that cultural training for the Alaskan (or any) Arctic environment should be provided to SOF and Conventional Forces prior to their arrival in their respective area of operations, the aspect of preparation in this area continues to meet with head-strong opposition. Personnel stationed in Alaska should be receiving training specific to Alaskan Native cultures on a regular basis as this knowledge is critical. As learned elsewhere, attempting to gain an understanding of a local Native culture *after* arrival in an area is a prelude to failure. This could be avoided by the implementation of training for forces well in advance. One would think that this lesson would have been learned by now.

Population - Identify and Address Grievances

As specifically related to Alaska, there are, unfortunately, remarkable similarities to Iraq and Afghanistan whereupon several facts should be recognized. The State, and the population contained therein, is very remote. It contains very mountainous, inhospitable terrain which is sometimes inaccessible even by air. The climate is harsh, and the weather is often unpredictable even in the best of circumstances. The State is a tremendous distance from the contiguous United States which, by default, makes immediate reinforcement of National Defense resources time consuming and sometimes nearly impossible. All of these factors result in the isolation of many portions of the population.

To reinforce the importance of understanding the human terrain is the much-needed recognition by planners, for current and future Arctic operations in Alaska, that there are number of tribal ethnicities (and associated cultures) calling Alaska their home. Alaska Native people "are divided into three ethnic groups, eleven distinct cultures, speak twenty different languages with more than 50 dialects, live in eight geographical locations in Alaska, in more than 200 villages and communities, and make up nearly 20% of the total population of Alaska."[24] Knowledge of this existing information must be captured and intensively studied by military forces operating in the US Arctic. It should also be information that is readily available and provided, well in advance, to any assisting foreign allies who might find themselves deployed to the Alaska AOR for training or in a worse-case event.

Many Alaskan villages and communities lie along the coast or in remote areas where the subsistence lifestyle has been commonplace for generations. In many of these locations, the villages are without critical infrastructure such as security or law enforcement, adequate healthcare, grid provided electricity, and in some cases, running water. Additionally, the people rarely, if ever, see representatives from the government (State or Federal) and any funding received is often limited. Education is commonly interrupted by the duties and responsiblities of the subsistence lifestyle which in turn, yields a statistically

---

[24] Information obtained from Alaska-Natives.com, "Alaska Native Cultures." Retrieved at: https:// www.alaskan-natives.com/alaskan-native-cultures/

high drop-out rate after 8th or 9th grade for those students who make it that far. An exceptionally high unemployment rate also exists, with little to no outside income from other sources, placing many of the families well below the poverty line when compared to other National and State averages. These are all easily identifiable grievances maintained by the population for extensive periods of time and they are grievances which are leverageable.

The absence of critical infrastructure, combined with the other issues identified, are grievances available for leveraging by our adversaries in order to sway the population away from favorable opinion of the USG and US forces. This should also be another lesson well learned from Iraq and Afghanistan in that recognizing and addressing grievances at the most basic level is critical to gaining and maintaining the much-needed support of the population. If COIN is considered to be "graduate level of warfare" as many have professed, then what has been readily identified in this, and the previous, paragraph should be considered COIN 101.

Compounding these identified issues further is the fact that there are some members in these remotely populated areas that maintain decades of long-standing disassociation with any type of governance due specifically to the continued neglect of historical, and generationally identified, grievances. This disassociation and the combined grievances are, again, issues available for our adversaries to leverage in order to sway opinion and support. It would be wise for the USG, Alaska State Governance, and US military to take a whole-of-government approach, through already proven IDAD concepts and practices, to address existing or long-standing grievances in order to eliminate the potential for future exploitation by any adversary. The question is, will they?

In *"A Leader's Handbook to Unconventional Warfare,"* author LTC Mark Grdovic references, *"A Basic Doctrine for the Conduct of Unconventional Warfare"* written by former Office of Strategic Services (OSS) and CIA veteran Frank Lindsay published in April 1961. On page 24 of LTC Grdovic's handbook, he relays in Lindsay's words (under the subheading of *"Compatible Goals and Ideology with Those of the United States"*) that one of the prerequisites identified and required for the successful prosecution of UW is:

"The goals of a resistance movement must essentially be Indigenous goals. It is unlikely that these goals will be identical with those of the United States.

Nevertheless, through the skillful influence of the U.S. representatives with the resistance leadership, a greater community of interest can be established, which will make it possible for the United States to provide assistance and to establish substantial influence over the course of the resistance itself. It is essential to recognize that the only goals and objectives that will provide sufficient motivation for a successful resistance are those that develop indigenously or are soundly based on Indigenous political and social conditions, and that goals and objectives artificially imposed from the outside will not find sufficient acceptance to make for a strong and successful resistance."

In the context of potential RO in Alaska (and anywhere else for that matter), the previous paragraph is of immense importance. While the US might have Nationalistic goals which they hope to achieve through the assistance of a resistance organization in a given area, the Indigenous population comprising the resistance organization might deem their long-standing community needs and grievances to be significantly more important than the wants, needs, or desires of the US government. Therefore, to align with what Lindsay states, the "Indigenous goals" far outweigh those of the US government and unless the US government can sufficiently address the grievances identified and assist the indigenous forces and population in meeting their goals, there is no motivation for the establishment of an Indigenous resistance or a partnership with the USG. What this means is that the localized goals of the people are far more important to them than are the Nationalistic goals of governance and country.

As already stated from an IDAD perspective, it would only be logical to follow already *proven and established* operational procedures implementing best practices learned overseas and applying them to remote Alaskan villages. As the USG deemed it beneficial to conduct FID, IDAD, and Security Force Assistance (SFA) programs in foreign countries during the Global War on Terrorism (before and since), the USG should also deem it beneficial to intervene and conduct similar programs specifically related to AHD (or Resistance Operations guidance) given the ever-growing threat identified in the Arctic Region. This approach is an extremely plausible consideration given that focus has rapidly shifted away from the US Central Command

(USCENTCOM) area of responsibility and only moderately, at this time, to the Arctic Region overall.

Concerted lines of effort should be made by the USG, Alaska State Government, and US military within these remote Alaskan communities. In return, community leaders will likely encourage community members to invest themselves not only in defense of their community, but also in defense of the State and the homeland (i.e., Nationalistic goals). All actions taken in remote communities by USG, State, and military forces must come with the endorsement of local leadership, both formal and informal. One excellent way, among many, to gain endorsements and trust from the leadership and the community as a whole is through methods of civil assistance such as that of a Medical Civil Assistance Program (MEDCAP) which the USG and State military forces can provide. As an alternative, National Guard medical units from the lower 48 States can be deployed during their annual training to conduct "real world" missions in remote areas of Alaska with liaisons from AKOM attached for key leader engagement purposes in those communities. This is not an "outside the box" perspective in any way. Rather, it is common sense approach to a real-world mission specifically for internal defense and developmental purposes.

Many remote villages and communities in Alaska maintain minimal medical capability solely in the form of a Community Health Aide (CHA). Any higher level of care is provided by a Physician's Assistant or Nurse Practitioner at the nearest regional medical clinic which could be many miles away as the crow flies, and then on to a regional hospital which is many miles away as a MEDEVAC plane flies. CHAs are trained in various medical skills to include some being Emergency Trauma Technicians as well as Emergency Medical Technicians. Gaining the endorsement and support of the Alaska Native Tribal Health Consortium, the organization that oversees the CHA program, would be of tremendous assistance in gaining confidence needed in USG efforts in remote areas. A USG sponsored MEDCAP, working in conjunction with the Consortium and local CHAs, would help to facilitate gaining the trust of the population as well as establishing forward medical support capabilities which is also an identified issue in Lt. Col. Hoettels article.

Relationships in remote areas cultivated through corresponding lines of effort and assistance could prove to be rewarding in the HD, RO, and Arctic

Strategy contexts. The support and trust of an organization such as the Alaska Native Tribal Health Consortium is one that could potentially influence the opinion of remote Indigenous populations while also being influential and impactful on efforts in other areas of mutual interest. Federal and State entities can easily implement these types of outreach programs across Alaska in order to aid in the development of remote communities while simultaneously forging relationships with the population and potentially gaining Indigenous support for future resistance operations.

Chapter 13

The Alaska State Defense Force

The Alaska State Defense Force (ASDF) should be an asset designated for Arctic domain awareness and other missions related to US Arctic Strategy; specifically, Resistance Operations and community leadership relationship building. While many States have a State Defense Force, Alaska's Force is unique in that it can be operationally relevant to US Arctic Strategy and the ROC immediately. The Force can further serve as an intelligence, surveillance, and reconnaissance asset, provide for domain awareness and sovereignty assurance patrols in remote areas, assist in search and rescue, and conduct critical infrastructure site surveys and area assessments. The force can do all of these things while simultaneously being an overall ground force multiplier. With their knowledge, skills, and expertise being of immense value, they are the primary "boots on the ground" in the US Arctic Region, the best asset for Arctic Homeland Defense, and the most immediate asset for building and training resistance forces in remote areas.

Alaska is a strategic location that is on the verge of finding itself in the middle of direct conflict, or conflict spillage, while also being a location where technological domain awareness assets will likely fail such as is discussed in both US Air Force and Army Arctic Strategy. Yet, as is often the case, the "people factor," or assets on the ground in remote locations, continues to be sacrificed for technology. People with specific skills and knowledge related directly to this type of environment are needed to accomplish difficult missions in the Arctic. Members of the ASDF have an Arctic Strategy enhancement capability, and they should be appropriately employed.

The unit currently maintains numerous remote operational locations across the State where the National Guard and other DOD components do not. One of these locations is *the* forward-most North American operational location of Little Diomede Island in the Bering Strait. Personnel on Little Diomede have directly observed, collected, and disseminated information regarding adversary activity for immediate relay to State Command personnel at Joint Force Headquarters located at Joint Base Elmendorf Richardson. This is but one advantage the Force provides in filling domain awareness information gaps, as defined by US Arctic Strategy, when the Alaska Air and Army National Guard and active component forces do not maintain the capability.

While individual branches of the US military have begun to slowly shift their attention to the growing tensions in the Arctic Region, the all-volunteer ASDF remains prepared for service but, it is an asset neglected. Even though they are a recognized organization of the State of Alaska Department of Military and Veterans Affairs, as well as an entity of the Alaska Organized Militia which also consists of the Air and Army National Guard and Alaska Naval Militia, the Force remains mostly omitted from inclusion in Arctic Strategy even by high-ranking officials in AKOM itself.

In contrast, other Arctic nations have recognized the necessity for assistance from their populations by actively seeking out specific knowledge and expertise. In fact, at least two other Arctic Nations have taken great strides to include the population in their resistance operations planning, preparations, and "Total Defense" concepts. But in typical US fashion regarding the Arctic Region, the US has fallen behind those Arctic allies as related to proactivity and preparation. Our Arctic allies plan and prepare accordingly while US strategists continue to accept the status-quo of permitting US Arctic vulnerability. This is an issue that, when considered, makes all NATO Arctic Nations vulnerable and the US a liability.

The ASDF is comprised of men and women with an ardent desire to serve their communities, their State, and their Nation. Most wear second-hand uniforms and boots that the State infrequently provides. Many pay for their own equipment, with no reimbursement, all while consistently devoting themselves to being the very first line of defense in keeping Alaska safe from harm when others cannot.

These men and women frequently take unpaid time-off from their jobs to attend unpaid weekend drills and annual and other training at their own expense. Unless placed on State Active-Duty status (Title 32), they make no money for what they do yet they participate in nearly all major State military exercises and have overwhelmingly responded to natural disasters and State emergencies. Even with all things considered, these personnel have repeatedly answered the call when members of the National Guard have sometimes, in all honesty, outright refused.

ASDF member prepares a shelter with Canadian counterpart while conducting domain awareness training in remote area of Alaska. Photo courtesy of ASDF.

Countless ASDF members have honed their survival and sustainment skillsets in the harsh Arctic environment for many years, far exceeding any military training provided to service members. Most know how to survive and thrive in both the Arctic and sub-Arctic environments of Alaska for extended periods of time because Alaska is their home, not just another duty station. They know, understand, and coexist with an environment that could very well be a frontline battleground in the near future. Many members are prior-service with combat experience as well as being avid Alaskan outdoorsmen and women such as hunters, trappers, dog-mushers, bush pilots, and anglers. Some reside in very remote areas of Alaska which provides for immediate access to a population where the US military has no presence. Without a doubt, these men and women are true patriots in every sense of the word.

ASDF members conduct combat water survival skills training.
Photo courtesy of ASDF.

In the unclassified version of the US Army Arctic Strategy (p.43), it is specifically stated that the Army is giving consideration to "Expand Arctic domain awareness through the potential creation of 'Alaska Scouts.'" Within this statement, it appears that the US Army has identified a need for such a unit as related to Arctic Homeland Defense. While the creation of this unit might seem new to some, it would actually be a re-creation of the previous 1st Alaska Scouts unit of WWII. A unit better known by the name of "Castner's Cutthroats."

"Castner's Cutthroats" were not your typical military members. They were rugged, rarely clean shaven, and projected a different military demeanor. They recognized that they had to coexist *with* their environment, not fight against it. These men had proven themselves highly capable of surviving in one of the most inhospitable environments known to man with Alaska Native tribe members, hunters, trappers, fishermen, and prospectors filling its ranks (just like the ASDF). Their backgrounds, and often generationally proven unorthodox methods of surviving, served the US Army tremendously well during the Alaska Campaign of WWII. These men were the original American Arctic Warriors, and the Army now recognizes their value once again. However, Alaska based unit leadership must readily acknowledge the value of these warriors and understand that they already exist on the ground in Alaska.

A Scout unit could provide the JFLCC and JFACC Commanders with invaluable capabilities due solely to being accustomed to operating in an Arctic environment for extended periods. Scout capabilities would be directly reflective of the needs identified in the Army and Air Force Arctic strategies while further possessing the ability to conduct unconventional warfare or resistance operations in denied areas if necessary.

A unit such as this would be highly advantageous to Special Operations Forces conducting missions in the Arctic of Alaska and could easily be created by assigning current State Defense Force personnel who would volunteer twice to serve in this capacity. Once a core group is established, as with its predecessor unit of WWII, members with unique skills in the Arctic environment should be actively recruited. This is especially true of those with language skills and cultural knowledge related to Alaska Native Tribes that can serve to assist SOF elements who will certainly find themselves operating alongside unfamiliar cultures in Alaska.

The ASDF can provide rapid assistance to multi-component and SOF with advantages in remote areas when technological or conventional assets will often fail due to identified Arctic related issues. Additionally, the Force can provide an "edge" to Arctic Strategy through its ability to conduct operations well in advance of the eventual arrival of SOF or larger conventional forces. A dedicated Alaska Scout unit from within the ASDF would be the only unit in Alaska that can provide this type of advantage since other units there do not maintain the capability to do so. As previously stated, the USAF Arctic Strategy states that, *"Interoperability is especially critical in the Arctic region due to terrain, limited access, and the low-density of domain awareness assets"* with this sentiment having also been echoed by the Army Arctic Strategy. Again, both strategies identify a knowledge gap and *a definitive need* for reliable domain awareness assets on the ground. These assets already exist in Alaska, but only if the Alaska Scouts are formed and if the ASDF is included in strategic planning and implementation.

The ASDF readily maintains the capability to produce information through applying combat proven area assessments for inclusion in the Intelligence Preparation of the Battlefield (IPB) and Cultural Considerations of the Operational Environment (CCOE) processes. Force members who reside in remote locations have immediate access to key formal and informal community leaders which is access that will be of utmost importance in that SOF and conventional forces will need it in establishing relationships and trust with the community for potential resistance building or unconventional warfare operations. As learned in both Iraq and Afghanistan, waiting until troops are on the ground to attempt to develop relationships, an understanding of native culture, customs, and languages yields predictable and devastating consequences. There simply should not be a failure to adequately plan in this aspect due to the multitude of historical lessons learned over the past two decades.

The ASDF must have the latitude necessary for "outside the box" conduction of operations to accomplish near difficult missions. Typical winter modes of transportation such as dogsled teams and snowmobiles are near required mobility for hunting and trapping, supply/re-supply, search and rescue, medical evacuation, and access to other remote villages and communities. The absence of the knowledge and experience maintained by current US Arctic forces specifically related to these annual customary modes of transportation in the Arctic exposes yet another vulnerability in defense capability and exhibits an enormous gap in preparation for extended operations in the Arctic environment.

Currently, additional ASDF capabilities consist of medical, water purification, intelligence, engineering, security force operations, cyber operations, scouts, domain awareness and sovereignty assurance, and domestic emergency operations. The unit's 2021 revised Mission Essential Task List (METL) is directly reflective of domain awareness and security operations and aligns with US Arctic Strategy by conducting scout operations, Arctic operations, performing security force operations, and performing critical site and infrastructure security.

Arctic Homeland Defense operations require funding and support and in as much, the ASDF should not be overlooked simply because it is an all-volunteer, mostly non-paid force. One might believe that the already extensive capabilities of the ASDF would be recognized, effectively utilized, prepared, and expanded. However, the Force continues to be neglected or impeded financially at nearly every turn. Military leadership at all levels must re-evaluate and re-write the Arctic Strategy in order to be far more inclusive of the ASDF. These men and women will be some of the first called upon to lead in communities across Alaska, be it by necessity or by choice, in areas where they could easily find themselves engaged in guerrilla or resistance operations.

The ASDF might very well be the "backbone" of the Resistance Operation Concept if they were to be appropriately utilized. However, in order to be recognized in this type of official capacity, the ASDF must overcome two obstacles. First, the ASDF must re-define its role so as to conclusively determine where force capabilities directly align themselves with the presented Army Arctic Strategy and the Resistance Operation Concept and second, there exists the continued issue of lack of funding and support for the ASDF that must be provided.

The ASDF should be closely examined and determined to be the entity that can provide the best and most immediate foundation for ground force multiplication or to lead resistance operations in a region which could potentially find itself in the midst conflict or occupation. If utilized in no other capacity, the ASDF should be highly valued as an indispensable domain awareness and intelligence, surveillance, and reconnaissance (ISR) asset. The ASDF can also assist multi-component forces with its ability to immediately begin conducting domain awareness patrols, sovereignty assurance operations, community vulnerability assessments in remote/strategic locations, and the establishment of relationships with village and local leadership through key leader engagements in locations where active or reserve component forces have yet to venture.

ASDF members maintain undocumented knowledge of remote travel locations and could provide guidance of how to enter into areas of perceived limited access through the utilization of trails and overland passes that are not identified on any map. Personnel can provide training in generationally proven

Arctic survival techniques not found in any manual or being taught at any professional military course. And as previously discussed, the unit maintains the ability to provide critical information regarding domain and situational awareness through the application of proven ASCOPE/PMESII and SWEAT-MUS-R-O[25] area assessments for inclusion in the IPB and CCOE processes.

Because of their ability to see the "Big Picture," a 2021 change in the ASDF unit METL brought the unit into direct alignment with DOD and Army Arctic Strategy. The revised METL of the ASDF is now as follows:

1) Conduct Scouting Operations
2) Conduct Arctic Operations
3) Conduct/Employ Security Force Operations
4) Conduct/Perform Critical Site Security

As previously stated, the issue of funding for the ASDF is a huge obstacle for the organization. Therefore, unified lines of effort should be implemented by the USG, Alaska State Government, and US military in training, equipping, and funding this organization (as if it were for FID purposes). This consideration is due specifically to what should be their required involvement with AHD operations during times of both emergency and defense.

L2A2 – Lead, Liaise, Advise, Assist

ASDF Land Component forces could find themselves being a critical component involved in ground force multiplication or resistance operations in the Homeland Defense aspect of the Arctic Strategy as well as also finding themselves thrust into leadership roles during a time of a natural disaster. With the existence of current ASDF unit capabilities, in conjunction with the possibility of creating new detachments and additional capabilities in other remote locations, ASDF maintains the ability to gain immediate access to, and gain the trust of, the population. The ASDF is the first line of defense and

---

[25] ASCOPE/PMESII is an acronym for: Area, Structures, Capabilities, Organizations, People, Events/Political, Military, Economic, Social, Information, and Infrastructure. SWEAT-MUS-R-O represents: Sewage, Water, Electricity, Academics, Trash - Medical, Unemployment, Security – Roads - Other.

timely information collection (as previously illustrated with the example of Little Diomede Island) in the event of either adversary aggression or natural disaster.

ASDF personnel have already demonstrated their advisory and leadership abilities and value in situations through direct L2A2 (Lead, Liaise, Advise, Assist) implementation. In 2022, numerous ASDF personnel deployed to both Nome and Bethel to work by, with, and through local leadership during emergent operations after disastrous flooding. Personnel implemented their L2A2 skills in the following ways:

1. Lead: They provided direct leadership and leadership support to local governance which presented with unity of effort during a time of emergency. ASDF personnel could also (if necessary) augment local leadership during times of crisis and emergency in accordance with local formal leadership requirements. Additionally, ASDF forces could provide leadership to an unorganized militia or guerrilla force if activated by the Governor, in accordance with Alaska Statutes, during a time of National Defense.
2. Liaise: ASDF personnel served as direct liaisons between local and State governance during a time of crisis and emergency. They could also serve as direct liaison on the ground between Active/Reserve component military units/personnel, local governance, and the population during a time of National Defense.
3. Advise: ASDF personnel advised local leadership during the event on best courses of action. They could also advise unorganized militia or guerrilla forces on best courses of action required or requested from Active/Reserve component military units in order to maintain unity of effort during a time of National Defense.
4. Assist: ASDF personnel were there to assist local governance by augmenting police forces (if had been necessary) during the emergency. They could further assist local governance by providing security for critical infrastructure during a time of crisis or disaster and assist local governance with establishing lines of communication if other forms (cellphones, landlines, internet) have been compromised or lost. ASDF personnel could also maintain alternate forms of

communication with AKOM Higher Headquarters for State/National Emergency Response.

The L2A2 concept has the potential for enhancement and additional value if there were to be direct involvement of Security Force Assistance Brigade (SFAB) advisory personnel. This could also be established through an internally developed training program constructed and instructed by personnel (both civilian and ASDF) who reside in Alaska that have been in advisory roles in either Iraq or Afghanistan (or both), and by those who have been instructors at the Foreign Security Forces Combat Advisors Course formerly located at Ft. Polk, LA.

As specifically stated in Army Training Publication (ATP) 3-96.1, *Security Force Assistance Brigade*, the core mission of the SFAB is to:

"...to assess, train, advise, and assist FSF in coordination with joint, interagency, and multinational forces to improve partner capability and capacity and to facilitate achievement of U.S. strategic objectives. This mission set is developed from the organize, train, equip, rebuild, and build, advise, and assist, and assess concept (known as OTERA-A) described in FM 3-22."

The very definition provided could easily be modified from "assist Foreign Security Forces (FSF)" to read, "assist Arctic Indigenous Forces." This would align with the US Arctic Strategy which would serve to complement achievement of the US Strategic objective of Homeland Defense in the Arctic (Alaska). Additionally, involvement of SFAB or internally trained advisor personnel would assist in allowing SOF units to focus their efforts in other areas of Arctic operations without breaking continuity of effort in remote areas or jeopardizing relationships established with the population.

Whatever the case, SFAB or ASDF advisory personnel should be deemed as necessary for employment within the context of Army Arctic Strategy and Homeland Defense. In an environment where building relationships with the population and understanding culture is of chief importance, advisory personnel working as dedicated detached teams or individuals in remote locations of Alaska would be a tremendous asset.

Strategic Partnering to Enhance Tactical Level Capabilities

A unique strategic partnership with AKOM Land Components could be developed if "outside the box" thinking is encouraged. AKOM partnership with an Army National Guard Special Forces Group such as the 19th Special Forces Group (Airborne) or smaller units of the newly activated 11th Airborne Division at JBER could provide several advantages within the context of the overall Arctic Strategy. A few of these potential advantages are:

1. The 19th Special Forces Group (Airborne) could be tasked to expand its AOR to include Alaska and align with shortcomings identified in Arctic Strategy analysis. Training could be provided to AKOM members which would expand domain awareness, security capabilities, creation of intelligence assets, and begin the conceptualization/realization of the Resistance Operations Concept as applied in remote areas.

2. Members of the 11th Airborne Division could be tasked with advisory roles and attached to AKOM in order to acquire knowledge from AKOM members related specifically to the Alaska region and to aid in information sharing. This would tremendously expand the knowledge base for homeland defense purposes and fill information gaps for Alaska based units.

3. Suggest that at least annual training for members of the 19th Special Forces Group (Airborne) could take place with conduction of real-world mission training of organized militia forces in unconventional warfare, internal defense, special reconnaissance (domain awareness and area assessments), resistance and/or guerrilla operations, communications, intermediate medical, and security force assistance. Members of the 11th Airborne Division would also benefit from receiving this training alongside their AKOM and SF counterparts to ensure continuity of efforts which align with Arctic Strategy.

4. Annual training during the winter months in the Alaskan Arctic would provide members of the 19th Special Forces Group (Airborne), the 11th Airborne Division, and AKOM with the opportunity to hone skillsets and receive cross-training in other professional areas such as advisory

and assistance operations as well as assessing their perceived state of readiness to conduct sustained operations in the Arctic.

The relationships between SOF, the 11th Airborne Division, and the ASDF should be highly encouraged. These relationships would serve to enhance defense and operational capability in the Arctic as well as provide training for the members of other units through instruction of "best practices" learned through first-hand experience.

Chapter 14

The Alaska Scouts

As was briefly discussed in the previous chapter, the US Army Arctic Strategy mentions establishing an Alaska Scout unit. This chapter will go into further detail about the potential of the Scout unit and who should maintain Operational Control (OPCON) of the unit.

Castner's Cutthroats in the bush. Retrieved from https://natesalaskanadventure.com/2016/05/24/castners-cutthroats/

Mission of the Alaska Scouts

The mission of a modern-era Alaska Scout unit would be similar to that of their WWII predecessors. The Scouts should be trained and employed as a lightly equipped, highly mobile asset fully comprised of those accustomed to operating in the Arctic environment.

The Scouts would possess the ability to train and lead small irregular forces in conducting asymmetric warfare in denied areas if possible. These asymmetric capabilities and a unit METL would include, but are not limited to:

1. Use of alternative mobility methods to access otherwise denied areas.
2. Downed Aircraft Recovery Teams, Search and Rescue of pilot/aircrew/sensitive equipment on aircraft.
3. Advise and assist other US military conventional and SOF elements in unfamiliar areas, especially with regard to the population and terrain.
4. Mapping of the Human Terrain for the ever-changing IPB and CCOE processes as this enhances domain and situational awareness per Arctic Strategy.
5. Call for and adjust indirect fire (as Forward Observers).
6. Target Identification for Long Range (Laser Guided) and/or Close Air Support.
7. Target Interdiction (Long range precision marksmanship).
8. Consideration of other resistance or guerrilla warfare-based methodologies involving small units in denied areas.

It is recommended that Indigenous forces such as the Alaska Scouts conduct missions in partnership with dedicated SOF and smaller Conventional Forces. When operating independently, Scouts should avoid enemy engagements whenever possible as theirs is not that type of mission. However, deliberate engagement in the form of long-range precision marksmanship could be utilized to neutralize a target of opportunity or when slowing enemy pursuit during a unit egress.

Operational Control and Funding

Operational Control (OPCON) of the Alaska Scouts should fall directly under the Department of the Army, Alaskan Command/U.S. Army Alaska (USARAK), or the U.S. Army Reserve. OPCON of the Scouts should not be assigned to the State of Alaska or AKOM. The justification for OPCON to Alaskan Command/USARAK is as follows:

1. The Alaskan Combat Intelligence Platoon/Company (Alaska Scouts) is a dedicated combat asset designed to operate in the most austere conditions in direct support of the AHD mission in order to enhance domain and situational awareness, conduct sovereignty operations, and enhance ISR capability in the Arctic of Alaska.
2. The Alaska Scouts should be recognized as an Organized Militia entity separate from all other AKOM elements. The unit should be specifically designed as an auxiliary reserve force for Title 10 activation during a time of insurrection or war in accordance with Article 1, Section 8, Clauses 15 & 16 of the U.S. Constitution and the recognized enumerated powers of Congress. The precedent set forth as a specific Title 10 entity supersedes the Governor's "at will" authority to activate this unit into State service in accordance with Alaska Statutes.

With the U.S Army specifically stating that there is consideration for creation of an "auxiliary force" in its Arctic Strategy, it is probable that the Army has also considered a way to provide funding for such a unit. Also, the Army's recognition of an organized auxiliary force would permit unit creation outside that of those currently existing units of AKOM. Funding for the Alaska Scouts should proceed as a line of effort for AHD operations from the USG and DOD. USARAK should provide strict oversight of the funding specifically for defense and development under established parameters specifically for the reason of Arctic Homeland Defense.

Leadership and Unit Organization

Command of the Alaska Scout unit should be assigned to someone who knows Alaska and has lived there for many years. A Reserve or Retired Colonel (O-6) or a former or current ASDF senior officer who understands Alaska, understands the uniqueness of the operational environment, respects the land, and respects the Native people and their cultures.

The Commander of this unit must be provided with the latitude necessary to accomplish seemingly impossible missions through his utilization of unconventional methods and relationships *specific* to the Arctic environment. He/she must be someone that is trained and proficient in small unit tactics, can teach those tactics to the subordinate members of the unit, can entrust that unit members can readily teach the tactics to resistance forces, and employ those tactics in an Arctic operational environment. He/she must be someone that not only commands respect from subordinates, but also someone who gives equal respect to subordinates regardless of rank. He/she must command these Asymmetric Arctic Warriors by example, never asking them to do anything that he/she would not do.

Decentralized leadership ideology within this organization should be encouraged considering the austere environment and independence in which the unit would conduct operations and the fact that this unit is anything but conventional. Historically speaking, a decentralized leadership style produced tremendous success for Finnish forces during their asymmetric Winter War of 1939-1940 against the invading Soviets. The leaders of Finnish forces operating at the tactical level were extremely successful in conducting guerrilla operations against the overwhelming opposition force numbers and equipment of the Soviets. The Finns were successful because they were encouraged by their leadership to think "outside the box" and employ unorthodox methods of warfare in an atypical environment.

The Arctic Region continues to emerge as one of the most highly contested regions of the world. As the situation escalates, the U.S. military would serve itself well if decentralized leadership were an encouraged and acceptable practice promoted within its ranks and *applied* by current and future leaders who might find themselves operating there.

In many ways, the already established all volunteer ASDF stands capable of rapidly transitioning select personnel to a Combat Intelligence and Advising Company or a Scout unit. As stated, there are just over 200 current members of the ASDF located in numerous communities across the State with over half of these members being prior military and many of those being combat veterans. Their positioning amongst the population provides access to the cultural knowledge of the Indigenous population, aligns directly with the Army Arctic Strategy, and enhances Arctic defense capability.

Chapter 15

The Arctic Guerrilla

When you hear the words "guerrilla warfare," what do you envision? Think for a moment. Where does your mind take you? It is likely that it takes you to the hot, miserable jungles of the Vietnam War where the Viet-Cong were a virtually invisible enemy who would emplace various punji traps or trip wired booby traps along their trails. Or it could be that your mind takes you to the mountainous and unforgiving terrain of Afghanistan where the Mujahideen waged nearly unrelenting guerrilla warfare against the Soviets for a decade and many of these same warriors, or their sons and grandsons, waged a similar guerrilla campaign against US and Coalition Forces for two decades until finally ousting them as well.

No matter where your mind might take you, there exists plenty of historical documentation of "lessons learned" related to guerrilla warfare. Simply by studying the Viet-Cong and their tactics in Vietnam, the Mujahideen tactics in Afghanistan, and Chechen tactics in their war with the Russians, volumes of documented history exist from which we should learn. Much can be learned from the literal stacks of documentation that we have at our disposal, from both "winners and losers," in the past 20 years alone, and much of what is learned can be applied should an Arctic conflict take place. But prior to doing so, we must first get past the stereotyping often associated with the guerrilla and his/her version of warfare.

Once considered to be "dirty tactics" employed by the enemy, guerrilla warfare has silently risen to the forefront of operations abroad. This is especially true in the Mujahideen efforts against the Soviets, the Chechens against the Russians, and most currently, "resistance" efforts against the Russians in Ukraine.

Most outsiders have simply not understood the effectiveness of "hit and run" or "swarming" tactics frequently utilized by guerrillas against much larger military forces versus that of standing and fighting honorably with their enemy in a force-on-force manner (insert "Front rank kneel" here). Guerrilla tactics have often been misperceived or mislabeled as cowardly, even during the American Revolution. However, it was not until a new generation of warfighters actually began to study the strengths and advantages posed by tactics of guerrilla warfare and resistance operations that a conscious shift among academics, military professionals, and policy makers began doing their part to change the historically propagandized mis-perceptions of this ancient form of war fighting.

As I personally began to delve deeper into the study of the subject in 2009, I began to comprehend how this "War of the Flea" is, and can be, effectively utilized in the much broader, though minute, scope. It was only through my study that I determined that resistance and guerrilla warfare is in fact an honorable war-fighting methodology. Well, that is to say depending on what side you are on.

As stated, much has been written on the subject and with the writings came the accompaniment of countless thoughts and opinions. As with most any topic, there are both pros and cons associated in addition to the valid reservations and considerations of those who wage guerrilla warfare out of necessity while there remain those who staunchly oppose the methodology altogether.

Over the course of time, guerrilla warfare methodology has been applied in both major and low intensity conflicts by many powerful nations (including the US). In fact, even major business organizations refer to some of their tactics as "guerrilla" when applied to their competitors. All of this has resulted in a "softening" of the terminology in order to align with political correctness, foreign and internal policy, and acceptance of guerrilla practices. In doing so, guerrilla warfare has now come to be known by less offensive terms such as "Asymmetric Warfare" or "Resistance Operations." In whatever manner it might now be identified by friend or foe alike, many of the tactics and techniques employed are still guerrilla by their very nature. As they say, one can dress the window any way they might like, but at the end of the day, it remains a window.

But what if a situation that required these actions were to arise on US or other allied soil? Would political correctness and softer terminology be considerations of the type of warfare that would be waged by the population against a foreign invader and occupier? In assessing this question, another must also now be asked. Could the politicians of every friendly Arctic Nation (primarily the United States) and NATO, as well as others of the United Nations sympathetic to the US, "stomach" some of the tactics often associated with the type of warfare that must be undertaken by the population? Remember these questions.

In his book, *"The Ethics of Insurgency: A Critical Guide to Just Guerrilla Warfare,"* author Michael L. Gross writes that:

"Guerrillas and insurgents must prove their worth. They must establish the justice of their cause on the same basis of national self-defense that gives states the right to fight and must prove themselves the legitimate representatives of their people's national aspirations."

While Gross' statement is reasonable, it is contended that a strong opposing sentiment would also be expressed by those being governed by an occupying force. It should be considered that not all people involved in conducting guerrilla warfare or resistance operations against an occupying force will feel compelled to prove their worth as legitimate representatives for the purpose of "national aspirations." This was discussed earlier with Maslow's Hierarchy of Needs.

Many will be more likely to outwardly express a powerful desire to protect their families and their way of life in the occupied area either out of necessity, through deliberate intervention or covert means, or caused by some type of direct or indirect alienation (the Accidental Guerrilla). In reality, most involved in a resistance movement would probably care less about proving their worth via patriotic exhibition to gain support for their cause, and even far less about national aspirations or a "cause" that was probably determined by some political ideology or desired end-state goals conjured up in an office far removed from the location of the actual occupation. The guerrillas would likely act more out of self-preservation associated with personal or familial survivability with national interest being far down their list of reasons to fight (reference Frank Lindsay's pre-requisite discussed earlier in conjunction with Maslow's Hierarchy of Needs).

According to Gross, and the justification provided as to why most might choose to get involved in a resistance movement against a foreign occupier, the answer to the first question in a previous paragraph is Yes, while the answer to the second in the same paragraph is No. First, it is apparent that political correctness must be presented, even when waging warfare against an occupying force, and the stigma associated with guerrilla warfare would still be a major point of contention for policy makers. Conversely however, the same policy makers *would* readily accept certain guerrilla warfare methodology/tactics but only through the expressed softening of terminology by labeling it as "Resistance Operations," "Partisan Warfare," or "Total Defense" just as we are currently witnessing in Ukraine. The acceptance of such is conveyed for nothing more than for the optics of the situation in the eyes of the global community. Positive optics provide the opportunity to obtain external support (funding, aid) for the national interest (as defined by politicians), *not for the actual civilian population* involved in direct conflict with an occupying force.

Examining the Resistance Operating Concept (ROC)

According to Otto Fiala, author of the ROC manual, he states:

"The primary focus of the ROC is developing a nationally authorized, organized resistance capability prior to an invasion and full or partial occupation resulting in a loss of territory and sovereignty. Resistance, as a form of warfare, can be conceived as part of a layered, in-depth national defense. Toward this end, the ROC first seeks to delineate the concept of national resilience in a pre-crisis environment. The ROC describes resilience as the will and ability to withstand external pressures and influences and/or recover from the effects of those pressures or influences. National resilience is enhanced with the formation of a national resistance capability. Second, the ROC seeks to develop resistance requirements, and support planning and operations in the event that an adversary compromises or violates the sovereignty and independence of an allied or PN. The ROC attempts to demonstrate both the significance of national resilience and the criticality of maintaining legitimacy during the conduct of resistance operations during the struggle to restore and resume national sovereignty."

As can be observed in this paragraph written by Fiala on page 1 of the ROC manual, he imparts that concept implementation and capability establishment should begin "…prior to an invasion or full or partial occupation…" as the ROC "first seeks to delineate the concept of national resilience in a pre-crisis environment." This statement implies that the concept must be implemented long before any potential near-peer adversary invades or occupies sovereign territory, to include Alaska. Attempting to implement such a concept post invasion or occupation is doomed as by that time, the population of the occupied area(s) will be difficult, if not impossible, to reach or organize.

Also written on page 1 of the manual, Fiala states that:

"The government and military, with popular support, take action against an enemy in a traditional conventional defensive environment. The population is the primary actor in a resistance or Total Defense situation. Allies and partners play a very significant role in supporting the resistance effort. The most significant difference between traditional and Total Defense is the preparation required to ensure that the population is ready to fulfill its Total Defense role. In a Total Defense construct, the population has an increased/greater, more significant role. This preparation is part of the resilience concept. Enhancing and institutionalizing collaboration among government ministries, civic organizations, and the larger public is critical to success. This collaboration helps build a more resilient society and strengthens resistance networks established in the event resistance is required."

In this paragraph, Fiala notes that the population is the primary actor, or defender in this case, in a situation involving adversary invasion or occupation. He also specifically states that the most significant difference between traditional and Total Defense is the *preparation required* to ensure population readiness and the further importance of required collaboration across government agencies and the population which "strengthens resistance networks established in the event resistance is required."

Of other significance in this particular paragraph is Fiala's opening sentence that, "The government and military, with popular support, take action against an enemy in a traditional conventional defensive environment." Aside from the fact that this will be anything but a traditional or conventional environment, this sentence generates two applicable questions which are related to the American and Alaskan populations. These questions are:

1. How can the concept be expected to succeed, when the population does not express popular support for the government and military due to disassociation from governance caused by governance? And,
2. How can governance (State and Federal) expect the populations of very remote areas in Alaska to assume the role of "primary actor" when many populations in those remote areas have long-standing, identified grievances over basic needs with government?

These two questions can be answered with the documented perspective of CIA Veteran Frank Lindsay. As presented in Chapter 12, Lindsay stated in 1961:

"The goals of a resistance movement must essentially be indigenous goals. It is unlikely that these goals will be identical with those of the United States. Nevertheless, through the skillful influence of the U.S. representatives with the resistance leadership, a greater community of interest can be established, which will make it possible for the United States to provide assistance and to establish substantial influence over the course of the resistance itself. It is essential to recognize that the only goals and objectives that will provide sufficient motivation for a successful resistance are those that develop indigenously or are soundly based on Indigenous political and social conditions, and that goals and objectives artificially imposed from the outside will not find sufficient acceptance to make for a strong and successful resistance."

As Mr. Lindsay candidly suggests, Indigenous goals of a remote population will likely differ tremendously from the goals of US politicians and US military leadership. When Mr. Fiala's statement is applied to the historical situation as related to tribes in the American Arctic, the US Government could potentially find that they are turned away by the local population in many areas when they are asked for their support.

It is also remarkably interesting that Lindsay chose the words, "skillful influence" as a necessity for US representatives in order to gain popular support of the resistance and obtain "sufficient motivation" necessary for establishing a resistance in a given area. Will US representatives be able to influence a population already so far geographically removed and politically and socially disconnected from any type of governance? Possibly, but not without skillful influencers first gaining access to the population, understanding the culture of that population, having key leader engagements, and the ability to change the perceptions of the population from that of long-standing grievances and localized goals to those of "greater community of interest" through commitment and follow-through on promises made. This has all been discussed in previous chapters and in essence, it will be a "one tribe at a time" approach by the USG and military forces. In alignment with Fiala's writings, this will be a time-consuming process that must begin long before any near-peer adversary decides to invade or occupy a portion of Alaskan soil.

Other Foreseeable Difficulties

If resistance/guerrilla organizations are organized in remote areas after skillful influencing by US representative, those operating in small communities will meet with their most difficulty in maintaining the secrecy that is necessary for the conduction of their activities and/or their organization as a whole. In again using the example of Nome, it is a small community even though it is considered by Alaskan standards to be more "city-like." Yet, it is a place where everyone in the community knows nearly everyone else, which potentially equates to everyone knowing everyone else's personal business.

In Nome, there also exists an overall lack of friendly terrain, beyond the city limits, for conduction of extensive operations. Nome proper presents with being a remotely "boxed in" community surrounded by very rugged and inhospitable terrain on one side and the ocean on the other. When the difficulties of accessing the surrounding terrain of Nome are compounded by the harsh winter weather annually experienced there, the conduction of extensive military or resistance operations in the area becomes impossible. If a resistance or guerrilla organization were to establish a base of operations anywhere outside of Nome proper, it would be highly unlikely that any offensive operations could be conducted against an adversary entrenched or embedded amongst the remaining population. The guerrillas themselves would face tremendous hardships involved with issues such as travel, potential civilian collateral damage, and primarily, survivability through the winter. This in conjunction with the fact that the enemy will automatically presume that the guerrillas are from the local community given that no other community exists in the immediate area.

If the resistance in any small community does somehow manage to maintain secrecy of their activities (the covert aspect), the conduction of harassing guerrilla operations such as raids, ambushes, or sabotage (the overt aspect) against an occupying enemy force would prove extremely difficult. This is perceived to be true given that remote areas in places like Nome (or similar) and their surrounding nearby communities have only so much real estate in which to operate. They are in essence "boxed in" as previously stated. Overt operations would draw immediate, unwanted attention directly to the small population and this attention would likely be accompanied by severe repercussions. Any repercussions against the local population suggest that <u>someone will eventually talk</u> about what and who they know in order to save their own life or the lives of family members. While someone talking might be viewed by others as sympathetic to the occupiers, a serious question should be asked. What might you do to save the life of your wife, your husband, your mother or your father, or your children in the event that a gun was put to their heads by a foreign occupation force commander demanding information? Would you talk then as well?

Statistically speaking, percentages are high that during the initial phase of the invasion, foreign enemy forces would eliminate *anyone* who attempted to defend the location or resist. Additionally, they would also attempt to confiscate all known weapons from the population, by means such as obtaining local records of guns sales like the ATF Form 4473, thereby demoralizing the will and means to resist. This is the perfect example of why resistance members operating in a small community would best serve the overall military and governmental efforts by covert means such as in an intelligence collection capacity as opposed to that of an overt fighting force. As will be discussed in the next chapter of this book, the potential for a decades old program to be resurrected exists which provides for the initiative to be seized upon in order to recruit and train resistance intelligence collection personnel. But with each passing day that the US Arctic Strategy remains neglected or stagnant, the initiative for such a program continues to be lost. This results in the US providing even more advantages to our near-peer adversaries in the Arctic.

Many people caught in occupied territory will want to become guerrillas out of anger. While it seems perfectly logical that most everyone will want to do their part in the initial stages, anger leads to overreaction and the undermining of future efforts. Anger will subside, and interest in immediate retaliation against the occupiers will eventually wane as the new "normal" begins to be established. As previously stated, conducting guerrilla operations in small communities could have devastating consequences for the local population as a whole, especially when conducted out of pure anger and emotion. Some will volunteer to serve as the leader of the group and insist that people join them in the fight, however, it is not wise to follow. A resistance leader will emerge when the time is right during the occupation, if not before, and he or she will be selected by their peers based on his or her actions leading up to, or during, the crisis. This fact is echoed in the old Army Field Manual, FM 31-21, *"Guerrilla Warfare and Special Operations Forces"* published in May 1958. In Chapter 3 of the manual, it states:

"Resistance by subjects of a regime begins with the desire of individuals to modify or end conditions imposed upon them by invasion, occupation or by an unpopular regime in their country. The feeling of opposition toward and hatred of conditions that conflict with the individual's values, interests, aspirations, and way of life spreads from the individual to his family, to close friends, and to neighbors. As a result, an entire locality may be obsessed with hatred for the established legal authority. Initially, it is spontaneous. As the discontent grows, "natural leaders", e.g., ex-military personnel, clergymen, local office holders, and neighborhood spokesmen emerge to guide it into channels of resistance and encourage its growth."

Neglecting to Implement the ROC

Currently, there has been a complete disregard to implement the ROC as part of both Arctic and Homeland Defense Strategy. Why? It is officially known that the threat is real as it was identified and stated by the Director of National Intelligence in the unclassified threat assessment provided in February 2022. In conjunction, Fiala blatantly states that it is the population who will be the primary actor in a resistance or Total Defense situation. Why then is the US Government not responding appropriately to engage, assist, advise, and prepare the population in Alaska? There is simply no logical reasoning for this.

Russia and many of its Arctic military assets are positioned less than 60 miles from the coast of Alaska across the Bering Strait. This distance is closer than the 90 or so miles that Cuba is from Key West, Florida and the 195 miles Cuba is from Miami. It is now also public knowledge that China plans to build a signals intelligence base in Cuba and position troops there. This fact should provide most any logical person with good reason to believe that some Chinese troops are probably already on the Caribbean island of Cuba now. Given that all of this information is public knowledge, not to mention cause for tremendous public concern to the people of South Florida, it should provide the USG with the motivation necessary to implement the ROC concept in specific areas of Florida. If that is to be the case, then why has it not already happened in Alaska? For more than 20 years Putin has been slowly reaching Arctic dominance and if there has ever been a place to implement a concept like the ROC, Alaska is that place.

Instead, the USG continues in its malingering efforts in the Arctic and doing so has placed the lives of hundreds of thousands of Alaskans at risk and directly in harm's way. If the USG continues along the same path related to Arctic Homeland Defense as it has since at least 2014, then Alaskans have been presented with no other choice but to take the initiative and prepare themselves for a fight which may have already covertly arrived. At this point, Floridians should probably begin contemplation of doing the same.

Organizing in the Absence of Government Support

In the continued absence of government support for the preparation and training of a resistance network in Alaska, deciding well in advance of any conflict to organize, or become a member in, a resistance or guerrilla movement is a serious individual decision. Prior to any decision being made, strengths and limitations should be identified in order to determine where your skillsets will best be utilized.

Most likely, an adversary/enemy force occupying a community such as Nome will already know who the key people are in that community as well as infrastructure capabilities. Key people will include the community leadership (formal and informal), doctors, leaders of community organizations, etc. as information related to these people is easily obtainable via the internet or by human intelligence collection gathered by embedded assets or provided by sympathizers on the ground well in advance. If you organize a resistance effort for preparation purposes, it is an innovative idea for you and other members to also know the key people are and the critical infrastructure capabilities of your community as well.

As stated, in small communities under occupation the underground activity of intelligence collection will be extremely important. If you consciously decide to take part in this effort, ask yourself questions such as: Who do you know and where do they work? What types of information do they have access to that they willingly discuss? What types of information or facilities do you currently have access to? How will this access be impacted in the event of an occupation? What type of information can you begin collecting now that would benefit friendly forces if you had the opportunity to turn it over to them? Do you know one person, no more, that you can trust with your life and your secret that you can "recruit" so as to begin assisting you in this endeavor? If a conscious decision to become covertly involved in a resistance effort is made, then these are some questions that you need to begin answering now.

An analysis of 2nd and 3rd order effects of network operations must be seriously assessed by everyone involved. How will covert operations or activities, if discovered or once known, impact the local population both directly and indirectly? This is an assessment that must be made long before any occupation might occur therefore, contingency plans must be developed in advance.

Another particularly important aspect that must be gauged prior to any potential occupation is the size of the resistance network in a given area. If it is decided to organize a group in advance, keep it small and keep it secret. In a place like Nome, with a population of 3,699 people, a recommendation of no more than 5-8 members would be sufficient. A group too large is a danger to everyone involved and the population. Remember, a secret is no longer a secret if everyone knows about it. Maintaining the secrecy of the organization and its activities is of utmost importance. As a leader of the group is selected and the decision is potentially made to "grow" the movement, everyone involved must be highly selective and critical of people who can be extremely trustworthy and those that have exhibited the ability to remain calm under pressure and keep secrets.

If another network appears in the same area within a brief period of time after occupation, maintain your secrecy and keep your distance. This could be a ruse being employed by the intelligence apparatus of occupying forces. Through the use of sympathizers, they will attempt to "draw out" anyone involved with a real or suspected movement. Anyone involved with the real network, one that should have been established long before any occupation, should present themselves as normal and as low-key as possible on a daily basis. Do not invite attention to yourself, but do not be a recluse either as this could arouse suspicion. Do not find yourself getting caught up in being invited to any sudden or special meetings where forming a resistance is the central topic to be discussed. Stay clear of these types of gatherings and maintain your assumed disassociation with the subject. You know what you are covertly doing, others do not. Keep it that way.

Train Now

Begin training in selected areas of expertise now whether that expertise is in emergency medicine, intelligence collection, information dissemination (operations), etc. For the purpose of this section of the book, I will expand on the example of underground intelligence collection.

If you choose to collect information, begin practicing information collection skills. People like to talk so let them. Learn how to be an effective listener and ways to ask questions relating to information you seek without them realizing you are actually doing so. "How's the job going?" "What do they have you doing over there?" If you know someone that works at the hospital, ask them questions about what type of illnesses or injuries they are seeing. "How many Covid cases do they have over there now?" "How many vaccinations have they given out now in town?" "Are you seeing a lot of cold weather injuries this year?' These are simple questions that seem harmless, but the answers can provide a lot of information and even confirm information which there might have been previous doubts about.

Go to a bar and sit back and listen to what others are saying. Alcohol induces bravado. Voices and conversations typically get louder after a few drinks and over background music. With that, information comes more freely when the right questions are asked and when the correctly timed and placed encouraging comments are made. An active listener easily obtains all of this information.

A resistance network intelligence collector in a small community should attempt to place his or herself into a position of employment where they have access to other people on a near daily basis. People and the knowledge they maintain are the primary sources of information. A hospital or medical clinic staff member, a bartender, a barber or salon technician, an electrician, or plumber, a grocery or sporting goods store employee, etc., are all occupations that involve a lot of social interaction with people that have information. Those working in these professions are also great people to know for information retrieval as well.

Another good place to collect information is at the grocery or drug store. Opportunities may present themselves to actively listen to two or more people engaged in conversation while casually walking past them in the aisle and browsing items on the shelf. The entire conversation will likely not be heard, but pieces of their conversation can be obtained. Those pieces may provide a general idea of the topic they are discussing which could be information of some value.

Any information of substance should be verified, whenever possible, with a secondary source however, do not intentionally disregard any information heard that could potentially be of interest. Try to commit information collected to memory, not to paper. It will be necessary at times to write down information such as dates, times, identities, what was said, and how and when it was verified but keep this information hidden somewhere that only you know about. If during an occupation by a foreign force, commit everything, as best as is possible, to memory. Write down nothing. Have nothing, get caught with nothing.

Do not overlook the opportunity of involving a trusted partnership with someone of the opposite sex in this endeavor. Excluding someone such as this could potentially limit obtainable information to only 50% of what might be out there. In acceptance of historical fact, there are things that men will only tell men and women will only tell women. This is especially true in the barber shop, the sporting goods store, the hair or nail salon, the locker room, and the respective restrooms at the bar. These are all typical locations where individuals will inadvertently let down their "guard" and disclose information about others when they are amongst their closest friends.

These are just a few information collection practices which can be practiced now and utilized during an occupation of foreign forces. And do not forget about the simple SALUTE report you can obtain on the occupation forces. Their unit Size, their Activity, their Locations, their known Unit identification, the Time of collection, and any Equipment which they are using. Though you might not speak the language of the occupiers, members of the community may have interactions with some of the occupiers or hear rumors about their forces that will be quietly or secretly discussed.

Generally speaking, most people simply are not good at keeping secrets. The urge to tell someone a secret typically consumes a person until they do. Training yourself to be an effective listener and learning how to keep a secret now could provide critical intelligence to pass on in the future if afforded the opportunity.

Chapter 16

The Arctic Guerrilla Intelligence Network

Alaska is a "hotbed" of foreign military intelligence activity in what could be described as the Last Frontier in the New Cold War. As of this writing, there have been numerous intercepts (those officially reported by NORAD) of Russian military aircraft since 2020 (and prior) off the coast of Alaska. Russian Navy vessels have openly operated in the international waters of the Bering Strait near Alaska and the Chinese Navy has even ventured there as well. As recently as May 2023, Chinese Nationals (spies) posing as tourists breached the security checkpoint of Ft. Wainwright leading to their apprehension. This, of course, is not to mention the "Chinese weather balloon" that floated over the State in conjunction with the shoot down of an "unidentified" object ten miles off the coast of Alaska in February 2023.

One must wonder if all of this combined upswing in Russian and Chinese military activity near Alaska's coast, in/near Alaskan skies, or on Alaskan soil, is due merely to their desire for Arctic expansion? Or could it be that the increased activity is something far more important to the long-game of both adversarial nations? These are questions which need to be answered.

What has failed to be recognized and presented to the American public, potentially due to the headlines of more ostentatious stories such as Russian aircraft intercepts, is that Alaska is replete with readily available US defense and critical infrastructure information specific to the State itself, US Arctic preparation, capability, and readiness. In the technology age where most any of this information can be obtained by a few simple keystrokes, along with downloadable satellite imagery from Google Earth or other software programs, there lacks apparent consideration that foreign intelligence services would also utilize "old school" collection methodologies in their efforts. Some examples as specifically related to "old school" collection methodology applied to JBER are:

1. Foreign adversary intelligence operatives could easily observe JBER aircraft taking off and landing from numerous vantage points around Anchorage for extended periods of time daily. The fact that these aircraft fly so low can provide information such as tail numbers,

frequency and duration of flights, directional flight patterns, or approximate response time capability for foreign aircraft intercepts off the coast.
2. On most any given morning or afternoon, a foreign operative sitting in their vehicle at the local strip mall area near a main gate to the base could easily discern traffic patterns, number of approximate Security Force personnel at the gate and their shift change times, times of arrival and departure of personnel for potential targeting of specific personnel, types of vehicle driven by the targeted personnel and the opportunity to follow them to an off-base residence, or approximate number of personnel in and out of the gate during main arrival and departure times morning, mid-day, or evening.
3. A foreign operative could simply peruse the JBER website which is full of information on topics such as the status of upcoming exercises as well as the current status of conditions on base.
4. A foreign operative could easily peruse the internet in various places to obtain information regarding units and leadership, approximate troop strength, unit capabilities and equipment, troop deployment numbers and locations, information on Alaska critical infrastructure, information on Alaska leadership (local and State), information on local and State capabilities to include law enforcement, and the list goes on and on.
5. And finally, there is always the possibility of "loose lips sinking ships" at local establishments where alcohol consumption frequently negates every OPSEC briefing ever attended.

All of the aforementioned possibilities must be considered in Alaska and what should result is an increased counterintelligence effort by government agencies. Effective measures and activities must be developed and implemented by the DOD, FBI, AKOM, and other agencies in order to detect/deter any active or passive intelligence collection activities by foreign operatives located in Alaska. We know they are here, but active US counterintelligence measures and activities are, in all probability, minimal at best in Alaska.

Resurrecting the Past

With Alaska having become the new "Berlin" of sorts during the re-kindling of the Cold War, there exists an opportunity to implement an updated version of a previously classified program specific to Alaska. This program was a joint creation of the Air Force Office of Special Investigations (AFOSI) and the FBI. It was known as "Operation Washtub."

The purpose of "Operation Washtub," as stated in "Index A (I. Purpose)" of just over 2,300 pages of currently declassified information concerning the operation, was:

"to provide for an organization within Alaska designed to obtain, collect, and transmit such intelligence information as may be of value to the United States in the event that Alaska or a part thereof is invaded or occupied by the armed forces of an enemy."

Index A, written in what appears to have been sometime around 1950, also specifically addresses some of the very same concerns noted in the current 2020 Air Force Arctic Strategy. As related, Index A (II. Scope) states:

"It is contemplated that the plan will be sufficiently flexible to be adapted to unpredictable exigencies and situations. Within the limits prescribed by authorities of the United States and those imposed by such problems as climate, terrain, availability or proper quantity of agents, and the ruthlessness and efficiency of potential enemies[26], this plan contemplates informational coverage throughout all Alaska and the islands adjacent thereto, including the Aleutian Archipelago."

The USG's opportunity to implement an updated version of "Operation Washtub" for Arctic Homeland Defense is not as difficult as it might outwardly appear. Some specialized training would of course be necessary in critical areas, as outlined in "Operation Washtub" Index A (VII. Training of Agents), and would be required for personnel however, the USG would not have to reinvent the program as a whole. As previously stated, there currently

---

[26] The "ruthlessness and efficiency of potential enemies" is taken by the author of this assessment to mean the ruthlessness and efficiency in obtaining information through interrogation of captured persons or prisoners taken from the local population and its leadership.

exists more than 2,300 pages of declassified documentation pertaining to the previous operation in existence from 1950-1959. These documents provide a "blueprint" to follow for development and implementation of a new program for inclusion into the DOD Arctic Strategy and for the purpose of Arctic Homeland Defense.

In initially recruiting personnel, AKOM already maintains personnel who could easily assume the role necessary for near immediate implementation. While military members of AKOM are likely the most suitable candidates for this mission, other personnel (civilians) accepting this role should be specifically recruited based on current professions or skillsets. All personnel must be strictly of civilian status to avoid conflict of interest with any military hierarchy. Due to this recommendation, it is further recommended that oversight of the program be provided by a civilian governmental agency such as the Alaska based field office of the FBI.

The implementation of a program such as this is highly advantageous to AHD in that it allows for access of denied and remote areas of Alaska. Additionally, if only one member of such a program resides in an area that is likely to find itself occupied by a foreign adversary, there exists an intelligence collection capability and liaison to friendly forces on the ground there if needed. Having even one dedicated intelligence asset in an occupied area is critical in providing timely information to US forces for future operations in an area of low-density domain awareness as outlined in current Arctic strategies.

The original "Operation Washtub" has been a subject of US intelligence history long forgotten by many. However, this section of the book contends that an operation of its kind is applicable and exceptionally warranted in our present time given the current conditions related to recognized adversarial threats in the Arctic Region and Alaska.

Cyber-Intelligence Cell

With modern technology has also arrived new threats. The State of Alaska should develop and maintain a dedicated Cyber-Intelligence Cell to meet the hybrid threats posed by our adversaries and their continued advancement in technological attack capability.

All aspects of cyber incident operations/management require sufficient funding if they are to be effectively accomplished by any organization. Federal funding for such a program could be obtained if allotted for defense specific to the homeland. As former President Trump himself said at the Republican National Convention, televised on 27 August 2020, "We will win the race to 5G and build the world's best cyber and missile defense, already under construction." The very words spoken by the former President imply the recognized necessity for funding to accomplish this mission of AHD under the auspices of National Defense spending.

The cyber-intelligence tasking should fall directly under the responsibility and oversight of the Alaska National Guard (and other DOD entities) given that both have the funding and manpower to meet the mission requirements and specifications. Other civilian entities should also be considered for this tasking in a layered, joint effort.

Medical Intelligence Collection

During the Soviet occupation of Afghanistan, it was reported that nearly 67% of all personnel who served there:

"...required hospitalization for a serious illness. These illnesses included 115,308 cases of infectious hepatitis and 31,080 cases of typhoid fever. The remaining 269,544 cases were split between plague, malaria, cholera, diphtheria, meningitis, heart disease, shigellosis (infectious dysentery), amoebic dysentery, rheumatism, heat stroke, pneumonia, typhus, and paratyphus." (Grau & Jorgensen, 2005).

Foreign occupiers will likely bring with them foreign illnesses and diseases that could have an impact on the local population. Conversely, the occupiers will also be exposed to local illnesses and disease as is exhibited during the Soviets time in Afghanistan. While vaccinations against many illnesses and diseases have been produced, they are not always 100% effective (i.e., COVID vaccines).

More often than not, there is at least one illness that always impacts people no matter where they go, even if only on vacation. That illness is commonly known as "Traveler's Diarrhea" which is typically accompanied by mild to moderate dehydration even when treated and remedied. Another common illness that frequently finds its way into a population that sees a significant upswing in outside visitors virtually overnight is acute upper respiratory infection which is easily spread through coughing, sneezing, or simple face-to-face interactions. Upper respiratory infections can lead to far more serious respiratory illnesses and complications which could potentially be deadly across a population if not discovered and treated quickly. These are both issues that can potentially impact the occupation force and their effectiveness of current or future operations and this is useful information to collect.

In the Army Field Manual (FM) 8-55, *"Planning for Health Service Support,"* Appendix F states:

"Medical Intelligence is that intelligence produced from collection, evaluation, and analysis of information concerning the medical aspects of foreign areas that have immediate or potential impact on policies, plans, and operations. Medical intelligence also includes the observation of the fighting strength of enemy forces and the formation of assessments of foreign medical capabilities in both military and civilian sectors."

Closely monitoring information related to illnesses or disease in an occupied area, and any statistical data associated, is important. This is also important as related to aspects such as the community water supply and the possibility of any contamination or poisoning. Capturing Medical Intelligence related to the status (fighting strength) of occupying forces and the impact an illness or disease (or other issues) is having on them, and the local population, can be passed to friendly forces for future operational planning purposes and/or liberation.

Obviously, the best locations to collect medical intelligence are the hospitals and clinics. If not already established as a worker in a medical facility, attempt to develop a friendship with someone who does work there and ask them from time to time how things are going. Do not make it overly apparent that you are attempting to gain information. Rather, ask questions in a manner which seems to outwardly express genuine concern for yourself, your family, and the community. People like to talk so be prepared to ask "leading" questions and effectively listen.

Do not overlook simple observations when walking around town. Pay attention to other issues such as trash collecting in the streets, inoperable sewage removal capabilities causing a grotesque odor, or even the physical appearances of people. Any of these direct observations, and many others, which are present in any community provides an opportunity for the spawning and spreading of serious illness or disease.

Collect information about the food supplies that are being kept and consumed by occupation forces and the population. What are the foreign forces eating? How frequently are they eating? Is the population being provided with food or are their supplies critically low? Is rationing taking place for both the occupying force and the population? If so, what items are being rationed? What is the plan to feed the population if the food supplies run out?

What about the water supply? Is water still available to the community due to intact infrastructure capability? If not, do the occupying forces have ample amounts of water? Where are they getting it? Do they have purification capabilities that they are utilizing? Are they providing water to the population? Observe if the potable water supply is being rationed to the population or if water is even available to the population at all. This information is critically important as the Russians managed to "weaponize" the water supply in Ukraine in hopes of forcing the population into submission (Landy, 2022 & Hussein, 2022). This is known as the "carrot or the stick" approach.

In the book, *"The Battle for Afghanistan: The Soviets Versus the Mujahideen During the 1980's,"* authors Mohammad Yousaf and Mark Adkin provide a lot of pertinent information in a single paragraph that was related to the Soviet occupation there. The information was provided by Soviet prisoners of the Mujahideen and presents useful information related to medical intelligence. As Yousaf and Adkin wrote:

"By and large the average man of the MRD (Motor Rifle Division) detested the war, had no enthusiasm for his task, was concerned only with surviving and going home. Living conditions were harsh. Even in Kabul, camps were often tented, with forty men living in each throughout the winter packed around a single stove in the centre [sic]. Those in the middle roasted, those on

the outside froze. Lack of hygiene and bathing facilities caused sickness, as did a vitamin-deficient diet. Many Soviets went hungry for much of the time. Their rations were insufficient in quantity and lacked variety. Rarely did they eat fruit or vegetables."

As can be seen, there is an abundance of useful information in this single paragraph exhibiting the psychological and physical conditions of many of the Soviet soldiers. Additionally, information related to their living conditions, their illnesses, their lack of personal hygiene capabilities, and their dietary deficiencies is also described. All of this is valuable medical intelligence, and it is tremendously important to friendly forces.

Any type of information that can contribute to an assessment of the physical and psychological wellbeing of both the occupying force and the population is important. If help does eventually arrive, they will need this information to assist with their operations and relief efforts in the area. Nothing related to medical intelligence should be deemed as unimportant and consequently, much can be deduced by information that does not overtly appear to exist.

Arctic Defense Studies Group-Alaska (ADSG-AK)

In October 2019, Alaska Senator Lisa Murkowski presented a proposal before the Senate for the creation of the Ted Stevens Arctic Security Studies Center. The proposal was also supported by the Alaska State Legislature, fellow Alaskan Senator Dan Sullivan, and Hawaiian Senator Brian Schatz. In December 2020, the proposal finally received approval and the Center was officially opened in June 2022. However, it is apparent that many at the facility appear to be more academically inclined to the research and study of other issues in the Arctic rather than to the subjects of security or National Defense. This fact overtly demonstrates a severe deviation from the intended purpose of a "Security Studies Center."

Without doubt, there is an immediate need for an "outside the box" approach to threat information assessment, collection, and analysis capability as specifically related to Homeland Defense, the Arctic, and the impact on Alaska. While the DOD has written multiple strategies pertaining to the Arctic, the Russians and Chinese have continued to grow stronger and more emboldened in their strategic positioning there. The fact that US Arctic

Strategy and policy continues to be slowly implemented is proving costly and the need for an independent organization or group, entirely devoted to <u>defense</u> information collection and analysis pertaining to the Arctic Region, should no longer be neglected.

The proposed ADSG-AK, or something similar in nature, should be a joint military-civilian advisory group created to collect open-source and classified information to conduct analysis on threat nations (Russia, China, North Korea) and threat activity as specifically related to Alaskan Arctic defense and the US Arctic Strategy. A group such as ADSG-AK should have the primary mission of actively monitoring the activities of threat nations in order to determine the impact on Arctic Homeland Defense. ADSG-AK information collected, along with reports produced, would provide timely and accurate information to DOD and AKOM entities as well as other governmental agencies. Information collected and analyzed via unclassified open-source methodology can be easily converted into classified intelligence products and disseminated as necessary for implementation at the strategic, operational, and tactical levels.

As stated, ADSG-AK should encourage open-source "outside the box" critical thinking and collection methodologies which currently are atypical at the new Ted Stevens Center. Through extensive analysis, logical conclusions should be ascertained to fill information gaps identified by US Arctic Strategy and Commanders. ADSG-AK can assist military commanders and defense officials with answering identified Priority Information Requirements and Commanders Critical Information Requirements directly associated with their missions and defense of the Alaskan Arctic Region.

Chapter 17

Arctic Guerrilla Medicine

During the progression of an enemy occupation, local conditions will deteriorate and with that, community capabilities will also decline. In addition to food and water shortages, medical treatment capability will begin to exhibit limited capability as well. During the initial invasion, there will no doubt be numerous civilian (and some invading force member) casualties that will quickly overwhelm the medical resources of the local hospital and clinics. Unless resupplied by the occupation force, there will be no immediate resupply to the hospital or clinics anytime soon. Chances are good that medical staff will be forced to work in their positions after the occupation as an asset to the occupation force. This means that civilians requiring any medical treatment will not be a priority. With this becoming the case, it will be important to identify trusted medical professionals, or those with previous medical backgrounds, who are willing to provide care outside of a hospital or clinical setting. This person, or these people, should be identified well in advance of a potential occupation by foreign forces.

The justification for receiving care outside of a clinical setting is based on the fact that resistance personnel simply cannot walk into any hospital or medical clinic in an occupied area with a severe injury due to the fact that the adversary will closely monitor these facilities. They will be looking for anyone coming in seeking treatment for wounds that might be out of the ordinary or suspicious. For example, a civilian with a gunshot, shrapnel, or a stab wound would arouse immediate suspicion *even if* it had been inflicted by an occupation force member accidentally or purposefully by another civilian. Another situation that could also raise suspicion would be that of numerous members of the civilian population (or even the occupiers) presenting with a sudden illness (i.e., upper respiratory infection or severe diarrhea) that could potentially impact the strength and capabilities of the occupying force. Be alert of this situation as many people presenting near simultaneously (within 12-24-48 hours) to a hospital or clinic with the same or similar symptoms of a known illness of unknown origin could result in the occupiers' efforts to eradicate the area of the illness by very authoritative means.

As stated, the guerrilla/resistance member must seek alternative, covert means of medical treatment in the event that it becomes necessary. Therefore, it is pertinent for the member to do two things:

1. Gain the confidence of a trusted medical provider, or at least someone with a medical background, who can provide treatment for minor, and sometimes even major, medical conditions often encountered in a conflict environment. And,

2. Maintain a firm comprehension of Self-Aid/Buddy Care and some advanced Combat Life Saving techniques and practices. The member does not need to be trained as an emergency medical practitioner such as an EMT or First Responder however, having basic knowledge of First Aid skills, combined with a few simple advanced skills in field medicine, should be sufficient in the short to mid-term.

First, finding a trusted medical professional and enlisting their services will not be easy. Once found, establishing trust might entail having to divulge the secrecy of your activity which may in turn have you attempting to recruit them into the network. It has been my direct experience in both military and civilian medicine that most advanced medical providers lose their people skills with patients and typically do not speak with them at length. This is especially true with civilian practitioners as "time is money" as they say. If they are under the terms of "conditional employment" at the hospital during the occupation, they may not wish to get involved with assisting in any way. However, this could change based on the personal circumstances of the provider and their sentiment towards the occupiers.

These people should always be considered needed only in the most emergent of situations and/or when all limitations of Self-Aid/Buddy Care and Combat Life Saving practices have been reached. This is done in order to maintain secrecy and provide protection for everyone involved. These would-be "guerrilla medical practitioners" might express   the cause but be cautious of those who are ove   be considered, and necessary, to inform the perso   ows about what you are doing, the better off they w   . T'   them with at least some sense of deniability if ever qu.   oned by occupation forces. If at all possible, offer some type of payment for their services such as food or water or whatever other items you might have to trade.

Second, maintaining the knowledge and confidence to provide Self Aid/Buddy Care, in conjunction with a few Combat Life Saver practices, will be immensely useful in an area of occupation. Not just for injuries which could be sustained during events against occupation forces, but for other minor injuries such as the most minute scratch or cut caused by sheer dumb luck which could eventually become infected and then septic without a higher level of medical care.

Maintaining the skills and knowledge to provide care for yourself or others for a short to mid-term duration will also be information that you can pass-on to many others. Not everyone has the knowledge of (or the stomach for) basic First Aid practices such as how to control bleeding, or splinting a fracture, or even understanding the difference between acetaminophen and ibuprofen and for what they are used. Learn medical skills in order to not only provide treatment for yourself in a time of need, but also for your family. Use the resources you have stocked up on first before you go to others (unless absolutely necessary) and expect them to use their supplies for your injury or your needs.

If you must go to someone else for assistance with an issue that is beyond what you are capable of handling, do your best to provide re-supply materials to them as soon as possible. In a situation such as an occupation, you never know how many other people might be seeking help from that very same person. Assisting that person with re-supply materials that you might have on hand, or may be able to acquire or make, will give you "street credit" with that person which may prove to be an incredibly good thing to have if needed.

In brief summary for Self-Aid/Buddy Care, do your best to provide your own care for yourself and your family without drawing any unwanted attention from the occupiers and the locals. Treat <u>every</u> medical situation under the assumption that help is not coming anytime soon.

As an additional note to this section, maintaining good personal hygiene should be obvious. This is an often-overlooked area of Self-Aid. Even though there may be restrictions on daily water consumption per household, do your absolute best to stay clean under the circumstances. If you cannot take a bath or shower daily, take a "bird bath" in the sink or utilize baby wipes for the process. Do what you can to maintain clean clothing and clean linen as this will aid in the prevention of lice. Open windows and allow the house to "air" out when possible. Exhaled air (CO2) trapped in enclosed living spaces occupied by 3-4 (or more) people becomes malodorous, stagnant, and conducive to illness. If you have disinfectants, use them as necessary while simultaneously doing your best to conserve your supplies. If the conditions of the occupied area are permissible, try to get outside each day for at least 30 minutes for a short walk, even if it is only in your backyard should you have one. At that point, it might no longer be the freshest of air, but some fresh air is better than nothing. Do your absolute best to stay clean and sanitary. Others in the community will neglect their personal hygiene and cleanliness of their living conditions and they will suffer for doing so.

Medical Experience

A guerrilla/resistance member who maintains medical skills can utilize those skills while simultaneously obtaining information from patients (the population) without raising suspicion. As conditions and capabilities deteriorate in the community, many people might determine that it is best not to go to the hospital or a medical clinic for treatment for any condition unless it is absolutely necessary (i.e., a life-or-death situation) and this provides an opportunity to interact with others and gather information.

As previously discussed, it would be wise for advanced planning purposes if the guerrilla/resistance member is capable of providing self-treatment whenever possible. It should also be acceptable that a person maintaining these types of skills and knowledge should assist anyone in need if safely determined. There are countless numbers of medical books available online (for free) or at the local library on First Aid, advanced First Aid, and even minor field surgery. It would also be advisable to obtain a comprehensive book on Wilderness Medicine that describes in great detail many not so ordinary injuries, illnesses and disease, and environmental injuries that could be encountered in a conflict environment where standardized medical care is either greatly reduced or not available. While the capability is available, watch videos online that show simple and common treatment practices for injuries or situations which might be encountered. Remember Murphy's Law, "Anything that can go wrong, will go wrong" so do not discount at least some basic knowledge of any medical or trauma event that you might think you will encounter in an occupied area.

Without doubt, local conditions and capabilities will significantly diminish under the occupation so keep the following piece of knowledge in mind. The occupiers will receive the best medical treatment *first*, even if provided by civilian population medical professionals, whereby the ability or need to treat the local population for even a common cold, or infection, or a traumatic injury will be secondary (if treated at all). While you may not be in the wilderness per se, you will be in an occupied environment that will no longer maintain capability of extended medical care or evacuation to a higher level of care. You have what you have to get through until friendly forces can liberate the area.

Stock-up On Medical Supplies

A good preparation idea is to have a stock of medical supplies (and knowledge of how to use them) in advance of any potential invasion or occupation by a foreign adversary. This is a just a good suggestion that holds true for any situation. The old saying of "it is better to have and not need, than to need and not have" is good advice when it comes to medical supplies.

What is stocked for medical supplies is really an individual choice however, there are some pertinent items that are strongly suggested to maintain. There are countless over the counter medications which can be purchased for many minor ailments such as diarrhea, nausea, motion sickness, fever, pain, allergy, sore throat, cough, and cold. Multi-vitamins are also a wise choice to invest in due to the fact that adequate food supplies and fresh vegetables will run critically short in an occupied area (as was encountered by the Soviets in Afghanistan as previously discussed).

It is highly recommended that, if possible, people obtain an excess of any daily prescription medications that might be needed. Antibiotics are an absolute "must have" if one can obtain them and stash them away in the event they are needed (there are legal, alternative ways to obtain these without a prescription, but I will leave that to your own research). As stated, an otherwise simple scratch can get infected to the point that it becomes toxic to the body and there may no longer exist the medical or pharmaceutical capability to curtail an infection's toxicity in an occupied area which means that death will likely follow.

It is also recommended that dental supplies be purchased along with other items such as bar soap, shampoo, deodorant, toilet paper, baby wipes, rubbing alcohol, Hydrogen Peroxide, Hydrocortisone cream, Neosporin, and Bacitracin. All are good things to have on hand.

For the ladies, it is a good idea to stock up on feminine hygiene supplies. An area under occupation will likely not receive any re-supply of these, and many other feminine needs, at the local grocery or pharmacy for an exceptionally long time. This means that sanitary alternatives will need to be developed so do some research ahead of time. Simply put, be prepared as supplies will eventually run out.

Putting together a quality First Aid kit for your home and family will go a long way in a situation such as an occupation, natural disaster, or civil unrest. Rubber gloves, gauze pads, Band-aids, athletic tape, duct-tape (yes, duct tape), Super Glue (yes, Super Glue), cotton balls, Q-tips, and a quality suturing kit (learn to do this, it is not difficult and instructional videos are available online). Hemostatic agents like Quik-Clot can now be readily purchased in most First Aid or outdoor sections of many local stores like Wal-Mart, CVS, Walgreens, etc. It is also advised that other bleeding control devices be maintained such as pressure dressings, a good tourniquet or two, and Ace wraps or bandages. Bleeding control devices can be easily made from common household items so learn how to make them.

Also maintain some water storage and techniques used expressly for water purification purposes. Inexpensive water purification tablets and devices can be purchased at most any retail store that maintains an outdoor or camping section. It is also wise to keep a couple of gallons of bleach in your stockpile and a printed copy or two of accurate measurements of utilizing bleach for the purpose of water purification. These measurements can be found online and should be placed with your purification supplies. Or you can always make your own water purification device which might be a comfort item that is nice to have. The video instructions for making one of these devices can also be found online.

The list can go on and on and what has been recommended here is by no means all-inclusive. The best suggestion is to go online and look at First Aid and medical kits (and other preparation supplies) that are being sold and then construct your own kit based on what they have in theirs. Imagine everything that you could potentially face in this worst-case scenario and build out a quality kit for you and your family.

Many, if not all, of the items mentioned can also be used as "currency." Yes, even a tampon may potentially have some value during an occupation in the same manner as medications, cigarettes, or alcohol. "Currency" comes in many forms during times such as these with high demand items being utilized during the trade and barter process and for future favors. Keep this in mind but keep the inventory of what you have in your stockpile a secret.

As a final piece of information to provide in this section, there is a website that I strongly suggest for everyone. It has countless articles written on about every medical issue that is likely to be encountered during a situation such as an occupation, a natural, or manmade disaster. The website is called *"Survival Medicine: Emergency First Aid & Supplies"* and was created and maintained by Dr. John Alton and APRN Amy Alton. Their site can be visited at https://www.doomandbloom.net/start-here/ and the amount of information on found there is staggering. Also included on their site is a direct link to their YouTube channel where numerous training videos can be watched. This should be an absolute "go to" resource for everyone reading this book.

Part III

Chapter 18
Amending Arctic Strategy

Without strong political support and unwavering dedication, US homeland defense in America's Arctic will remain vulnerable. Currently, there exists only a handful of politicians in Washington (and even Alaska) who recognize the imminent threat posed by our adversaries through the Arctic avenue of approach. Even less is the number of politicians who have more than a passing interest in the situation and the increasing danger presented to Alaska and the homeland.

With US focus having rapidly shifted away from the CENTCOM area of responsibility, politicians at all levels of government should now be encouraged to re-focus and engage on the Arctic with just as much fervor as they have done with Ukraine and Taiwan. This is necessary in order to understand that the threat is real, as the DNI stated, and that their political involvement is essential. Politicians need to further understand that the possibility of future conflict in the Arctic Region will impact US sovereignty, either directly or indirectly, due to that of spillage from other locations such as Ukraine and possibly Taiwan.

In order to address the lack of US preparation, readiness, and effectiveness in the Arctic for any short/mid/long-term conflict, the US must review, amend, and adhere to strategies set forth. Deviation from strategy exhibits indecision which is a vulnerability available for adversarial exploitation. In order to first amend strategy, it is strongly suggested that policy makers closely examine the following:

1. Understand why our adversaries would desire Alaska.
    - What are the vital natural resources and why would they be wanted?
    - Which location provides for, or maintains, the current infrastructure necessary for the retrieval of desired natural resources in the short/mid/long term?
    - Which location is most logical to obtain?
    - Which location would provide for easier expansion and the defense of the operational areas by our adversaries?

- Which location provides adversary advantages?
- Which location is best for further establishment and security of the Northern Sea Route?
- Where are the bulk of Russian Arctic Forces now geographically located?
- What location, if occupied, is more sustainable to long-term goals based on their current Arctic military strategy and capabilities?
- Which location, if occupied, would be easier to defend based on current military capabilities?
- Which location has a current US military defense capability, that is least prepared to conduct immediate/short/mid/long-term operations in a harsh Arctic environment?
- Which location would be more likely to produce a minimal response by the population to oppose an occupation?
- Which location would be more likely to produce an international response (external support) in order to support oppose an occupation?

2. Understand the number one priority of the National Defense Strategy which is Defense of the Homeland (p. 43. Army Arctic Strategy).
    - Must not only comprehend the "What," but also the "Why" of this priority.

3. Understand that regaining Arctic dominance must be done through Alaska first (the homeland) via credible deterrence as a first line of HD in the region. This approach is in direct alignment with the NDS' number one priority. (pp. 6-7, 43. Army Arctic Strategy).
    - Working "outside to inside" exposes homeland vulnerability for adversarial exploitation.
    - Must place more emphasis on the US strategy locally and nationally before globally.

4. Understand that Alaska is an intelligence collection "hot-spot" for foreign adversaries. It must be recognized that Alaska has become the Last Frontier in the New Cold War and is providing adversaries with

a "treasure trove" of intelligence through means including, but not limited to:
- Publication of unclassified Arctic Strategy.
- Publication of online articles specifically related to US Arctic military readiness.
- Publication of online videos/photos specifically related to US Arctic military training and exercises.
- Open-source information pertaining to critical infrastructure.
- Adversarial leveraging of population (civilian and military) for information and public support.
- Active and Passive intelligence collection.

5. We should seek internal (Indigenous) knowledge first. Each battlespace is different and applications of Arctic Warfare specific to Norway or other Arctic nations are not always going to be applicable to Arctic Homeland Defense in Alaska. An example of this is US leadership expecting the COIN successes in Iraq to be easily transferable to the COIN efforts in Afghanistan with the hopes and expectations of the same results. This simply did not happen due to tremendously differing operational environments and cultures.

6. Understand that Joint Force Warfare must include irregular forces constructed from the Indigenous population. "Joint Force" cannot simply mean a coalition of strictly NATO or Arctic allied military forces for Arctic Warfare and Arctic Homeland Defense. (p. 43. Army Arctic Strategy)
    - Must enhance the capability to defend the homeland by/with/through the support of the local population and indigenous irregular forces.

7. We must obtain the knowledge and guidance of the Indigenous population of Alaska as they know how to fight, survive, and thrive in the Arctic Operational Environment of Alaska.
    - Should create Indigenous Alaska Scout unit (pp. 5-6, 43. Army Arctic Strategy).

- Should employ the services of the local population for knowledge of the operational environment.

8. We must understand Alaska Native, and adversary, cultures, and conduct a thorough CCOE assessment for inclusion in IPB.
    - Should conduct extensive ASCOPE/PMESSII assessments of vulnerable areas or Alaska.
    - SOF and Conventional Forces must understand the Human Terrain to include potential adversaries.

9. We must recognize that any potential conflict in the Arctic will involve asymmetric or guerrilla warfare. We must plan appropriately for the implementation of resistance operations methodology of conducting warfare in denied areas through recognition of the following:
    - The Arctic itself is an asymmetric environment due to the harshness of its very nature and can prove advantageous for both friendly forces and adversaries alike. Early recognition of such should be a critical consideration during planning and conduction of operations by Special Operations and Conventional Forces.
    - Decentralized leadership styles should be promoted considering the austere environment in which units will find themselves conducting operations. The US military would serve itself well if decentralized leadership were an encouraged and acceptable practice promoted and *applied* by current and future leaders who might find themselves operating in denied areas of the Arctic.
    - As has been historically learned during our involvement in Iraq and Afghanistan (among other places), the population of Arctic areas will again be the center of knowledge and gravity. This involves a comprehension of the Native cultures (Number 6 above).
    - In remote areas of Alaska, populations are vulnerable to adversarial Information Operations Warfare and leveraging

due to maintaining decades of long-standing grievances and disassociation with governance at the State and Federal levels.
- In remote areas of Alaska, there should be conducted an extensive SWEAT-MUS-RO assessment as an initial attempt to address grievances. An assessment will reveal key information as well as to encourage face to face interaction with local populations and leadership through Key Leader Engagements.
- Arctic Strategy should include early and consistent key leader/community engagement with the population of identified vulnerable areas in order to gain and maintain their trust and support as is necessary for Arctic Homeland Defense.
- A combined effort of State, Federal, and Military leadership must get into these communities and establish working relationships through whole-of-government projects to assist the communities as defined in Joint Publications 3-22 and 3-27. If these efforts (both financial and physical) can be applied to FID as written, they can certainly be modified and applied for the specific purpose of Arctic Homeland Defense in Alaska.

10. We must admit that our adversaries know that current US Arctic military capability (preparedness, capability, readiness, and effectiveness) is minimal at this time and will be for several years to come. This fact is presented in Arctic strategies (to include the NDS) and many other published resources.

11. We must understand and admit that deployment of Arctic assets from Alaska into other geographical regions outside the State could prove to leave Alaska with even less than adequate defense capability. There should be an intensive study of the region(s) identified for possible Arctic deployment with achievement of at least some knowledge of those regions specified for Arctic operations. This can also be applied to HD. Knowledge such as:

- Existing (if any) military or resistance capabilities of the Host Nation region prior to deployment of US forces.
- Medical intelligence specific to the Host Nation and how issues could impact US forces deployed there as related to force sustainment.
- Identification of capability gaps (i.e., alternate means of access to remote areas, alternate means of transportation, communications, logistical support, etc.)
- The people and their culture.
- Terrain and climate considerations.

12. US political support must be obtained, maintained, and dedicated for the specific purpose of the implementation of Homeland Defense operations in the US Arctic.

Neither politicians nor military brass alone can change the current US Arctic Strategy. It requires both working together to accomplish the same goal. Unfortunately, the achievement of setting a common goal will require time. What will take even more time will be the fact that politicians and military leaders will have differing ideas on the way forward for defense in the US Arctic Region. Unless both factions can reach a mutual understanding that Homeland Defense in the US Arctic should be the primary concern, the issue will continue to take a "backseat" to other less important issues like global warming or questionable "security studies" there.

At the end of each day, it is problematic that most disagreements and conversations concerning the US Arctic will conclude that other intensive studies there are far more important than National Defense. Meanwhile, the Russians and Chinese are still progressing towards their goal of complete Arctic domination while the US remains all but absent, even with the slow implementation of current strategy. This absence continues to place American lives at risk in the Last Frontier which highlights the fact that efforts and strategy must change. As the DNI said in 2022, "The threat is real."

Chapter 19

Conclusion

The United States continues to find itself in a time of uncertainty and providing the foundation of that uncertainty is a population that is extremely divided due to numerous reasons. In the past two and a half years alone, we have experienced the coronavirus and the deaths associated, the further division of the population due to COVID-19 mandates and vaccinations, lockdowns and restriction of movement, unemployment, loss of income, the issue of defunding law enforcement, indecision of leadership, disinformation campaigns being promoted through media propaganda, a continued crisis at the US/Mexico border, civil unrest in several major US cities, and the botched withdrawal of US forces from Afghanistan for which no one has taken responsibility. In conjunction with aforementioned internal issues have been external issues such as the Russian invasion of Ukraine and the escalating tensions between China and Taiwan, China and the US, and Russia and NATO. All external issues have served to strengthen the ties between Russia, China, North Korea, and Iran in direct opposition of the United States.

With the US having nearly all of its attention focused on so many internal and external issues, conditions are giving way for the coming of a "perfect storm." Yet the storm is aptly being concealed by countless conditions which have been fueled by our near-peer adversaries in order to distract the US and NATO. Within the concealed storm, is the opportunity for a foreign nation (or nations) to exploit our weaknesses and vulnerabilities to their advantage in the Arctic Region and expand their dominance through bolder incursions.

As extensively discussed, it is unlikely that a Russian or a Russian-Chinese invasion of Alaska would include the whole of the State. Execution for an invasion of such magnitude is neither logical nor relatable to what is perceived to be immediate Russian or Chinese interests or goals in the Arctic Region. Instead, it is far more reasonable to believe that key strategic locations would be occupied while others (including Alaska military facilities and critical infrastructure) would be targeted by foreign forces with key terrain and weather being utilized to their strategic, operational, and tactical advantages. The elimination of selectively targeted US strategic locations in Alaska would assist in obtaining a "foothold" for enemy forces with their primary objective being that of occupying vital areas in order to retrieve many of Alaska's natural resources and establish both near and far side control of the Northern Sea Route.

I personally find it very unlikely that Putin would desire to fight a war on two fronts, meaning both Ukraine and in the Arctic. However, if China invades Taiwan and US forces are committed there from USINDOPACOM (inclusive of Alaska based forces), then Alaska would be extremely vulnerable to adversarial incursion. Likely, the bulk of NATO would remain occupied with the war in Ukraine and if the US gets drawn into a war with China over Taiwan, the already degraded defensive situation in Alaska might be a very tempting opportunity for both Putin and Xi. Possibly, it would present as an opportunity far too good to pass on which could result in Putin taking a gamble to re-claim a portion of land that was once Russia's to begin with while still being engaged in Ukraine.

History often repeats itself, as they say, so it is not surprising to say that in many ways, we have been here before. We face a historically old adversary, the "Russian Bear," who along the way has acquired a new ally in the "Chinese Dragon." The difference this time is that we have only minimally prepared to square-off against these highly formidable foes under some not so familiar circumstances in an asymmetric Arctic battleground. It is certain that climate and technology have changed over the decades, and will continue to do so, giving way to new strategic approaches and possibilities in Alaska and throughout the Arctic. However, the "game" remains the same. It is a game comprised of great power struggle and competition, now in the Arctic, with a "danger close" potential of conflict on US soil.

For over two decades, America has sat idly by and observed what has transpired in the Arctic Region. Some portions of strategy and planning developed many years ago might still be of some applicability even today if combined with new considerations for inclusion in the current Arctic Strategy. However, the problem for the United States in the Arctic and Alaska has always been the wavering commitment to the region which has been overtly apparent from the 1950's to the present day. This evidence coincides with the fact that American policy makers and military strategists never are remotely interested in planning for potential conflict in America's own backyard. "It could never happen here" as they say. In fact, it did happen here in the Aleutian Islands during WWII and on 11 September 2001.

There continues to exist the endemically false misconception that the mere creation and publication of Arctic Strategy is demonstrative of capability, readiness, power, effectiveness, and deterrence that US forces maintain for operations there. In concomitance, is the additional misconception that the creation of an Arctic Strategy, which includes Homeland Defense as the number one priority, equates to the readiness or preparedness necessary to *defend* the US homeland. But for many, including those who are in positions to implement change but instead choose to remain silent, it is widely well known that the US homeland is vulnerable through the Arctic avenue of approach, that is to say Alaska. If we know this, then we should be certain that the Bear and Dragon know it as well.

So, what if even half of the previous assertions of this book is true or even partially true? What if US forces are ill-prepared for a prolonged fight in harsh Arctic conditions as is openly discussed in various US Arctic strategies and as spoken to in countless videos online? What can be done? Who will fight the foreign invaders if they come to US soil when US military forces are absent from an area? Who will maintain the ability to conduct critical intelligence collection for US and NATO forces and then provide the information to them if presented with the opportunity? Who will be called upon to pick up arms, or sticks, or rocks, or spears, or bows and arrows to provide for Homeland Defense in the moment of need? The answer, obtained through logical deduction and substantiated by Mr. Fiala in the ROC manual, is the population.

But a resistance network cannot do it alone. They need support, and they need preparation and training. It is time for leadership to cease being reactive and inattentive to the situation in the American Arctic and follow the lead of other Arctic nations and the advanced preparations they are making with their populations in the event of war. The Swedish Government's Swedish Civil Contingencies Agency, for example, provided all 4.8 million homes in Sweden with a 20-page pamphlet titled *"If Crisis or War Comes"* (Time, May 2018) and can be accessed and downloaded for free online. In this pamphlet the "Total Defense" concept is discussed and how everyone, during a time of war, is "obliged to contribute" to the cause. Further discussed in the section of "Total Defense" is the topic of "If Sweden is attacked, resistance is required."

This is an exemplary way to prepare the population and express the government's need for their assistance. However, Sweden was not alone in their approach to the population.

Just days prior to Sweden's release of their pamphlet, Norway unveiled their own 100-page document, *"Support and Cooperation: A description of the total defence in Norway"* co-written by the Norwegian Ministry of Defense and Ministry of Justice and Public Security. This document addresses a broad range of topics related to total defense and the population. As with the document form Sweden, this one is also available for anyone with a computer to access and download for free.

If these two documents are not enough, and even if they are, it is highly suggested that the reader download the "Resistance Operating Concept (ROC)" published by Joint Special Operations University in 2020 written by Mr. Otto C. Fiala. This publication can also be obtained for free online and is yet another document full of valuable information. It is suggested that this manual be read from cover to cover and any video presentations by Mr. Fiala available online should also be watched. Upon reading this manual, anyone should be able to readily identify that this has been the "playbook" for what has been, and currently is, taking place in Ukraine against the Russians with the support of NATO.

All three of these highly recommended resources contain a lot of pertinent information with additional documents also contained therein that many have never been thought about. Certain items in these resources are as applicable to our daily lives in the event of a natural disaster just as they are also applicable in a time of war or another crisis.

The point of presenting these resources was to generate movement amongst an Alaskan population who has been kept in the "dark" as to what is taking place. Additionally, the resources were also provided to promote two questions for the Alaskan people to begin asking themselves. The questions are:

> 1. If other Arctic nations would publish these specific types of informative documents related to the Total Defense of their homelands and for their populations, why would the United States and Alaska not do the same for at least its population that resides in the

Arctic Region of Alaska? Russia has significant military assets positioned across the Bering Strait, with some being less than sixty miles away from the Alaskan coastline. And,

2. Why would the US military, US government, and Alaska State Government be so opposed to taking a proactive and whole-of-government approach in preparations related to the "Total Defense" or "Resistance Operations" concepts by at least providing resources to those populations of Alaska who reside inside of, or near, the Arctic? The people of these areas should be among the first prepared and trained for the event of war with the Russians and/or Chinese on US soil.

It is no secret, given all of the information readily provided in the current Arctic Strategy, that the near entirety of the US military is neither prepared, nor trained, nor equipped for extended operations in any Arctic environment. However, there are those who live, work, and play in the environment that have the knowledge, skills, and abilities to survive and thrive there. They can assist in mid to long term operations against a foreign adversary if needed and they are critical assets which should be included, not ignored, for the "Total Defense" of the US homeland.

For those who live in Alaska and have taken the opportunity to read this book, the time to rely on others for training and preparation in the event of a worse-case scenario in the Alaskan Arctic has passed. It is obvious, in the last five years alone, that US politicians and policy makers only raise the occasional eyebrow about Homeland Defense and the Arctic of Alaska. Clearly presented with the occasional eyebrow raising is the messaging that "no help is coming." In the absence of government concern and leadership, the time has come to seize the initiative and act in the event that it just might be necessary at some point to defend your family, yourself, your State, and our Homeland.

As both the Russians and Chinese continue to progress in the Arctic, they will become ever more emboldened in their actions due specifically to the lack of US commitment to, and military capability and preparedness in, the region. If help does eventually arrive, it could be months or years away and the duration of any assistance may be both logistically and time constrained. Ask yourself, are you prepared to do nothing and wait that long if you and your family find yourselves in an occupied area? Are you willing to place the safety and security of your family in the hands of people you have never met while waiting for a period of days, weeks, or months hoping that they are coming soon? Think about this.

Should you decide to initiate or take part in organizing and preparing a resistance movement in your community, download and read the manuals that have been discussed above and draw from the references and resources at the end of this book for more information. After conducting your own research, then decide where you can concentrate skillsets and how they can be utilized if needed. If you decide to include your family members in your decision and they are supportive, welcome them into the fold but keep in mind that <u>all of you</u> must keep everything "closely guarded," even with your best friends and even if they are a part of the resistance group.

Start organizing, planning, preparing, and training now in the event that you find yourself caught up in this type of potentially horrific situation. As part of your preparations, accept the fact that you are going to be in it for the "long-haul." If you consciously decide to do this, do it for the right reasons and decide what measures you must take to ensure the survival of your family and yourself as "priority one." Is it better for you to covertly collect intelligence or offer medical assistance as part of the underground effort when needed, or do you prefer to be a guerrilla fighter with an obviously shorter life expectancy against an overwhelming adversary force in a very isolated environment? What decision is best for your family? Only each individual can decide.

An additional suggestion that I also offer for Alaskans reading this book is to contact ASDF personnel if they are in your area. You do not have to join their ranks unless you desire to do so, but at least meet with the local members. Have coffee with them and discuss the current state of affairs in your area. Become friends with them as most are from the area (especially in remote locations) where they meet. Be supportive of their cause as you just never know when you might find yourselves in need of each other's mutual assistance. If no ASDF members are in your community or village, reach out to the organization through social media or a phone call to see how you can establish an active detachment in your community. If this is not possible, start talking with others in your community and develop contingency plans. If you have an established search and rescue group within your community, this might be a good topic to discuss with them and add to your capabilities.

In closing, if you make a commitment to resistance, then figure out how you are going to keep your family safe and live through it all, those are the primary goals. The secrecy surrounding what you will be doing is the "key" so never freely give it to anyone who does not have a need to know. Remember, the Swedish pamphlet states that everyone is obligated to contribute, I will add to this and close. While everyone should feel obligated to contribute, not everyone is obligated to know *how* you might be doing so.

From the Author

I do not profess to have all the answers, or any, and I have in no way presented myself as being a subject matter expert in this field or any other. It was important to share some of my background (at the end of the book) in order to provide justification as to why I felt qualified to write it. Like so many other Americans and Veterans, I bluntly ask the tough questions to our leaders and expect that our leaders should respect us enough to provide the answers to any tough questions posed. I feel that answers to tough questions should be provided even when the truth is difficult to present. As Americans, we all have a right to know.

I have been an active student of Insurgency, Counterinsurgency (COIN), and Guerrilla Warfare (GW) since 2005. As an early integral part of my "education" on these subjects, I spent a year in Iraq (Mosul and Baghdad) where I served as both a Combat Medic and Intelligence Analyst. During a portion of my time there, I was assigned as a Combat Medic to a Military Transition Team (MiTT) in Mosul consisting of a cohesive team of Army personnel that I had never met. True professionals, every one of them. Upon my arrival to the team, they all readily accepted me as a member of the team without question and afforded me an opportunity to gain invaluable knowledge and experience. Little did I know that the knowledge I obtained during my "crash course" in combat advising with the MiTT would be applied repeatedly even all these years later.

Upon returning from Iraq in July 2006, I was stationed at Ft. Dix, NJ for approximately two years where I trained Soldiers preparing for their deployments to both Iraq and Afghanistan. While at Ft. Dix, I began to expand my existing knowledge of Insurgency, COIN, and GW as well as share what I had learned to that point. I was initially assigned as a member of a six-person training team that developed and instructed the COIN training program for First Army and then co-assigned to the training Brigade Medical Detachment which served to train deploying medics in new skills being used "downrange" and instructing non-medical personnel in Combat Lifesaver skills.

After departing military service in November 2008, I was recruited for a special Department of the Army project and soon became a Federal Employee. Shortly after attending some very intensive training, in July 2009 I found myself in the middle of the counterinsurgency effort in Afghanistan. After a knee injury sent me home from Afghanistan in November 2010 for surgery and recovery, I attended the Foreign Security Forces Combat Advisor's Course at Ft. Polk, LA as a Federal civilian. After graduation from the Advisor's course, instead of returning to Afghanistan, I decided to leave federal employment and remain as a Defense Contractor involved with curriculum development and course instruction primarily for Insurgency and Counterinsurgency (in addition to other advisory skills). The men and women I worked with at Ft. Polk were all "top notch" and highly skilled.

In 2012, I went to Africa for private contract work with the State Department where I continued to apply the skills acquired from my study and application of the subjects mentioned above in yet another foreign culture and environment. Along with four other ex-pats in Mozambique, we recruited, trained, equipped, and "stood-up" a local guard force of just over 400 Mozambiquan personnel in just under 90-days. The men I worked with on this mission were outstanding and, as with the MiTT in Iraq, I learned a lot from all of them.

In February 2013, I relocated to Alaska and once again found myself working cross-culturally in the Yukon-Kuskokwim Delta in Bethel. After relocating to another location within Alaska, I finally settled in and called Alaska my home. Since 2017, I have been actively monitoring the Russian and Chinese situation in the Arctic and how the actions of the two nations are impacting Alaska and Homeland Defense. In mid-2020, I continued to further my knowledge in Unconventional Warfare, and corresponding subjects, to also include the current "flavor of the month" being utilized in Ukraine, the Resistance Operating Concept. When all has been said and done to date, the knowledge and practical experiences gained over a near 20-year period have been utilized to produce this book. However, I contend that this work is far from anything final.

This section has not been included in order to provide the reader with a "run-down" of my resume. It has simply been included to present why I felt qualified to write this book, nothing more. Like the book or hate it, keep the book, or discard it, if you might have learned just one thing from what I have written, then I deem the book to have been a success. Thank you for taking the time to read it. ---LSL

Acronym Glossary

ADSG-AK – Arctic Defense Studies Group-Alaska

AFOSI – Air Force Office of Special Investigations

AG – Arctic Guerrilla

AHD – Arctic Homeland Defense

AKOM – Alaska Organized Militia (Air/Army National Guard, ASDF, Alaska Naval Militia)

AKANG – Alaska Air National Guard

AKARNG – Alaska Army National Guard

AKNGJS – Alaska National Guard Joint Staff

ALCOM – Alaska Command

ANM – Alaska Naval Militia

AO – Area of Operations

AOR – Area of Responsibility

ASCOPE – Area, Structures, Capabilities, Organizations, People, Events

ASDF – Alaska State Defense Force

CA – Civil Affairs

CCOE – Cultural Considerations of the Operational Environment

CENTCOM – US Central Command

CF – Conventional Forces

CHA – Community Health Aide

CI – Counterintelligence

COE – Contemporary Operational Environment

COIN – Counterinsurgency

COMPACAF – Commander, Pacific Air Forces

COP – Common Operating Picture

CULINT – Cultural Intelligence

DA – Department of the Army

DAF – Department of the Air Force

DMVA – Department of Military and Veterans Affairs (Alaska)

DNI – Director of National Intelligence

DOD – Department of Defense

DON – Department of the Navy

EMP – Electro-Magnetic Pulse

EO – Exercise Objective

ETHINT – Ethnographic Intelligence

EWD – Early Warning Detection

FBI – Federal Bureau of Investigation

FID – Foreign Internal Defense

FOB – Forward Operating Base

GCC – Geographic Combatant Commander

HD – Homeland Defense

HIARNG – Hawaii Army National Guard

HN – Host Nation

HTA – Human Terrain Analyst

HTS – Human Terrain System

HTT – Human Terrain Team

IBCT – Infantry Brigade Combat Team

IDAD – Internal Defense and Development

IO – Information Operations

ISR – Intelligence, Surveillance, Reconnaissance

IPB – Intelligence Preparation of the Battlefield

IW – Irregular Warfare

JBER – Joint Base Elmendorf Richardson

JFACC – Joint Forces Air Component Command

JFLCC – Joint Forces Land Component Command

JP – Joint Publication

LIC – Low Intensity Conflict

LNO – Liaison Officer

MANPADS – Man-Portable Air Defense System

METL – Mission Essential Task List

MiTT or MTT – Military Training Team or Military Transition Team

NAVNORTH – US Navy North

NG – National Guard (Air NG, Army NG)

NORAD – North American Aerospace Defense Command

ODA – Operational Detachment Alpha

OE – Operational Environment

OGA – Other Government Agencies

OPCON – Operational Control

OPSEC – Operations Security

OTERA-A – Organize, Train, Equip, Rebuild/Build, Advise-Assess

PMESII – Political, Military, Economic, Social, Information, Infrastructure

PSYOP(s) – Psychological Operations

RO – Resistance Operations

ROC – Resistance Operating Concept

SALUTE Report – Size, Activity, Location Unit Identification, Time, and Equipment

SC – Security Cooperation

SF – Special Forces

SF GRP – Special Forces Group

SOCNORTH – Special Operations Command North

SOF – Special Operations Forces

SOF-LE – Special Operations Forces Liaison Element

SWEAT-MUS-R – Sewer, Water, Electricity, Academics, Trash-Medical, Unemployment, Security-Roads

TACON – Tactical Control

TAG – The Adjutant General

TRADOC – Training and Doctrine Command

US – United States

USARAK – US Army Alaska

USEUCOM – United States European Command

USAREUR – US Army Europe

USARPAC – US Army Pacific

USCG – US Coast Guard

USG – US Government

USINDOPACOM – US Indo-Pacific Command

USN – US Navy

USNORTHCOM – US Northern Command

USSOCOM – US Special Operations Command

UW – Unconventional Warfare

Resources and References

Alaska Community Health Aide Program. Retrieved from: http://www.akchap.org/html/home-page.html

Alaska Department of Military and Veterans Affairs, Alaska National Guard. 2021-2024 Strategy by Major General Torrence Saxe, The Adjutant General. Obtained through anonymous source collection, 2020.

Alaska Department of Military and Veterans Affairs Strategy, 2016 by Laurie Hummel. Former Adjutant General of the State of Alaska. Obtained through anonymous source collection, 2020.

Army Training Publication 3-96.1, *"Security Force Assistance Brigade."* May 2018. Retrieved from: https://armypubs.army.mil/epubs/DR_pubs/DR_a/pdf/web/ARN8448_ATP%203-96x1%20FINAL%20Web.pdf

Barron, Laignee. 2018. "Sweden Advises It's Citizens to Prepare Wet Wipes and Tinned Hummus in the Event of War." *Time.* 22 May 2018. Retrieved from: https:// time.com/5286505/sweden-war-preparation-pamphlet/

Berliner, Jeff. 1989. "Military Reports 253 'Brim Frost' Injuries." *UPI.* 3 February 2918. Retrieved from: https://www.upi.com/Archives/1989/02/03/Military-reports-253-Brim-Frost-injuries/7142602485200/

Berthiaume, Lee. 2020. "Canada, U.S. have lost military edge over Russia in the Arctic: NORAD commander." *The Canadian Press,* 13 February 2020. Retrieved from https://www.msn.com/en-ca/news/world/canada-us-have-lost-military-edge-over-russia-in-the-arctic-norad-commander/ar-BBZYja5?li=AAggFp4)

Bradley, D. (Director). (2012). *Red Dawn* [Film]. Contrafilm.

Christian, Patrick James. *Tribal Engagement: History, Law, and War as Operational Elements.* Florida: Universal-Publishers. 2011.

Cleveland, Charles T. *The American War of Irregular War: An Analytical Memoir.* Santa Monica, CA. RAND Corporation. 2020.

Cohen, Rachel S. 2021. "Spike in Russian Aircraft Intercepts Straining Air Force Crews in Alaska, Three-Star Says." *Air Force Times.* 28 April 2021. Retrieved from: https:// www.airforcetimes.com/news/your-air-force/2021/04/28/spike-in-russian-aircraft-intercepts-straining-air-force-crews-in-alaska-three-star-says/

Coll, Steve. *Ghost Wars*. New York: Penguin Books, 2005.

Davidge, Ric 2020. "Upgrading our Arctic Defenses." *The Alaska Roundtable.* August 5, 2020. Retrieved from: https://secureservercdn.net/198.71.233.47/n5q.11d.myftpupload.com/wp-content/uploads/2020/08/8_6_20-Upgrading-our-Arctic-Defenses-.pdf

Defense Intelligence Agency. "The Airborne Troops." Page 55. *Russia Military Power Report 2017.* Retrieved from: https://www.dia.mil/Portals/27/Documents/News/Military%20Power%20Publications/Russia%20Military%20Power%20Report%202017.pdf?ver=2017-06-28-144235-937

Department of the Army Field Manual 3-0, *"Operations,"* October 2022. Army Publishing Directorate. Retrieved from: https://armypubs.army.mil/epubs/DR_pubs/DR_a/ARN36290-FM_3-0-000-WEB-2.pdf

Department of the Army Field Manual 3-05.130, *"Army Special Operations Forces Unconventional Warfare,"* September 2008. Retrieved from: https://fas.org/irp/doddir/army/fm3-05-130.pdf

Department of the Army Field Manual 3-05.137, *Army Special Operations Forces Foreign Internal Defense."* June 2008. Retrieved from: https://info.publicintelligence.net/USArmy-ForeignInternalDefense-2008.pdf

Department of the Army Field Manual 3-05.202, *"Special Forces Foreign Internal Defense Operations."* February 2007.

Department of the Army Field Manual 3-22, *"Army Support to Security Operations,"* January 2013. Army Publishing Directorate. Retrieved from: https://armypubs.army.mil/epubs/DR_pubs/DR_a/pdf/web/fm3_22.pdf

Department of the Army Field Manual 3-24, *"Counterinsurgency."* Paladin Press. December 2006.

Department of the Army Field Manual 3-24 MCWP 3-33.5, *"Insurgencies and Countering Insurgencies."* May 2014. Retrieved from: https://armypubs.army.mil/epubs/DR_pubs/DR_a/pdf/web/fm3_24.pdf

Department of the Army Field Manual 3-24.2 *"Tactics in Counterinsurgency."* Sections 1-8 through 1-10. April 2009. Retrieved from: https://fas.org/irp/doddir/army/fm3-24-2.pdf

Department of the Army Field Manual 7-98, *"Operations in a Low Intensity Conflict."* 19 October 1992. Retrieved from: https://www.bits.de/NRANEU/others/amd-us-archive/fm7-98%2892%29.pdf

Department of the Army Field Manual 8-55, *"Planning for Health Service Support."* Army Publishing Directorate. September 1994.

Department of the Army Field Manual 31-16, *"Counterguerrilla Operations."* Army Publishing Directorate. February 1963.

Department of the Army Field Manual 31-21, *"Guerrilla Warfare and Special Operations Forces."* May 1958. Retrieved from: https://ia600206.us.archive.org/5/items/FM31_21_1958/FM31_21_1958.pdf

Department of the Army Field Manual 31-22, *"U.S. Army Counterinsurgency Forces."* Army Publishing Directorate. November 1963.

Department of the Army Field Manual 34-130 *"Intelligence Preparation of the Battlefield."* July 1994. Retrieved from: https://fas.org/irp/doddir/army/fm34-130.pdf

Department of Defense Joint Publication 3-22, *"Foreign Internal Defense."* 17 August 2018. Retrieved from: https:// fas.org/irp/doddir/dod/jp3_22.pdf

Department of Defense Joint Publication 3-27, *"Homeland Defense."* 10 April 2018. Retrieved from: https://www.jcs.mil/Portals/36/Documents/Doctrine/pubs/jp3_27.pdf

Fanning, Mary, and Alan Jones. "The Perfect Storm: Port Canaveral's Gulftainer Tied to Russia's 'Club-K' Container Missile Launcher, Jafar's Iraqi Nuclear 'Beach Ball,' North Korea, KGB Primakov, And Iran Deal as Russia Enters 'Endgame'." *The American Report.* October 27, 2017. Retrieved from: https://theamericanreport.org/2017/10/28/the-perfect-storm-port-canaveral-gulftainer-club-k-russia-endgame/

Fanning, Mary, and Alan Jones. "Russia's Pearl Harbor 2.0 Asymmetrical War Plans, Gulftainer, Club-K, and EMP." *Center for Strategic Policy.* October 24, 2018. Retrieved from: https://www.centerforsecuritypolicy.org/2018/10/24/russias-pearl-harbor-2-0-asymmetrical-war-plans-gulftainer-club-k-and-emp/

Federal Bureaus of Investigation. "Operation Washtub" documents, 1627 pages. Retrieved on 19 February 2020 from www.theblackvault.com

Federal Bureau of Investigation and US Air Force Office of Special Investigations. "Operation Washtub" documents, 705 pages. Retrieved on 19 February 2020 from www.theblackvault.com

Fiala, Otto C. 2020. "Resistance Operating Concept (ROC)." *Joint Special Operations University.* April 2020.

Fratus, Matt. "Operation Washtub: How Alaskans were trained in a Top Secret 'Stay Behind' Program During the Cold War." June 25, 2020. Retrieved from: https://coffeeordie.com/operation-washtub/

Fry, Nathan CPT. 2014. "Survivability, Sustainability, and Maneuverability: The Need for Joint Unity of Effort in Implementing the DOD Arctic Strategy at the Tactical and Operational Levels." *Military Review,* November-December 2014.

Grau, Les & Jorgensen, William. 2005. "Beaten by the Bugs: The Soviet-Afghan War Experience." *Military Review.* December 2005. Retrieved from: https://www.sovietarmy.com/beaten-by-the-bugs-the-soviet-afghan-war-experience/

Grdovic, Marc LTC. *A Leader's Handbook to Unconventional Warfare.* US Army John F. Kennedy Special Warfare Center and School: Special Warfare Professional Development Publication Office. 2009.

Gross, Michael L. "The Ethics of Insurgency: A Critical Guide to Just Guerrilla Warfare." University of Cambridge: Cambridge University Press. 2015.

Henley, Jon. 2018. "Sweden distributes 'be prepared for war' leaflet to all 4.8 million homes." *The Guardian.* 21 May 2018. Retrieved from https://www.theguardian.com/world/2018/may/21/sweden-distributes-be-prepared-for-war-cyber-terror-attack-leaflet-to-every-home

Hickman, Kennedy. 2019. "The Winter War." *ThoughtCo.* 3 April 2019. Retrieved from: https:// www.thoughtco.com/winter-war-death-in-the-snow-2361200#:~:text=The%20Winter%20War%20proved%20a%20costly%20victory%20for,Finns%20numbered%20around%2026%2C662%20dead%20and%2039%2C886%20wounded.

Hoettels, Elizabeth A. L., Lt. Col., USAF. (2023). Medical Support to the DoD Arctic Strategy. *Æther: A Journal of Strategic Airpower & Spacepower,* Vol.2, No. 1, Spring 2023. Retrieved from: https://www.airuniversity.af.edu

Hussein, Hussam. 2022. "Russia is Weaponizing Water in its Invasion of Ukraine." *Nature.* 29 March 2022. Retrieved from: https://www.nature.com/articles/d41586-022-00865-2

Kilcullen, David. *"The Accidental Guerrilla. Fighting Small Wars in the Midst of a Big one."* Oxford University Press. 2009.

Kilmeade, Brian. 2020. "Commander of USNORTHCOM and NORAD on intercepting Russian aircraft." Interview with General Terrance J. O'Shaughnessy. *Fox News,* 9 April 2020. Video 4:38. https://video.foxnews.com/v/6148333223001#sp=show-clips

Landy, Jonathan. 2022. "How Water has been Weaponized in Ukraine." *Reuters.* 22 October 2022. Retrieved from: https:// news.yahoo.com/water-weaponised-ukraine

Laruelle, Marlene. *Russia's Arctic Strategies and the Future of the Far North.* New York: M.E. Sharpe. 2014.

Lopez, C. Todd. 2019. "NORTHCOM Commander Cites Arctic as Area of Concern." *US Department of Defense/US Fed News Service,* 23 July 2019. Retrieved from https://www.defense.gov/Explore/News/Article/Article/1913989/northcom-commander-cites-arctic-as-area-of-concern/

McFate, Montgomery. 2005. *"Does Culture Matter? The Military Utility of Understanding Adversary Culture."* Retrieved from: e-mapsys.com/Cultural_Matters.pdf

McLeod, Saul. 2023, "Maslow's Hierarchy of Needs." *Simply Psychology.* 7 June 2023. Retrieved from: www.simplypsychology.org/maslow.html

McNamara, Robert S. with VanDerMark, Brian. *In Retrospect: The Tragedy and Lessons of Vietnam.* New York: Random House, Inc. 1995.

Meakins, Joss. "The Other Side of the COIN: The Russians in Chechnya." *Small Wars Journal.* January 13, 2017. Retrieved from: https://smallwarsjournal.com/jrnl/art/the-other-side-of-the-coin-the-russians-in-chechnya

Milius, J. (Director). (1984). *Red Dawn* [Film]. United Artists.

Montgomery, Nancy. 2018. "Military frostbite, cold weather injuries up with little explanation why." *Stars and Stripes.* 21 December 2018. Retrieved from: https:// www.stripes.com/military-frostbite-cold-weather-injuries-up-with-little-explanation-why-1.561535

Norway, 2018. Support and Cooperation: A description of the total defence in Norway." *Ministry of Defence and Ministry of Justice and Public Security.* 8 May 2018. Retrieved at: https:// www.regjeringen.no/contentassets/5a9bd774183b4d548e33da101e7f7d43/support-and-cooperation.pdf

Office of the Under Secretary of Defense for Policy. *"Report to Congress: Department of Defense Arctic Strategy"* June 2019. Retrieved from: https://media.defense.gov/2019/Jun/06/2002141657/-1/-1/1/2019-DOD-ARCTIC-STRATEGY.PDF

Person, Daniel. "The FBI's Top-Secret Plan to Defend Alaska from Communists." *Outside.* February 2, 2015. Retrieved from: https://outsideonlinecom/1930301/fbis-top-secret-plan-defend-alaska-communists

Pickrell, Ryan. "US general says NORAD responded to more Russian military flights near Alaska last year than any year since the Cold War." *BusinessInsider.* March 16, 2021. Retrieved from: https:// www.businessinsider.com/general-russian-military-flights-near-alaska-since-cold-war-2021-3

Pirro, Jeanine. 2014. "Lights out: The Danger to the US Power Grid." *Fox News,* 24 February 2014. Video retrieved from: https:// www.youtube.com/watch?v=nbRnJTm_o58

Raftsjo, C.W. 2018. "Tactics vs. Intelligence: Explaining Finnish Effectiveness in The Winter War." Retrieved from: www.researchgate.net/publication/327176788_Tactics_vs_Intelligence_Explaining_Finnish_Effectiveness_in_The_Winter_War

Rearden, Jim. *Castner's Cutthroats: Saga of the Alaska Scouts.* Pictorial Histories Publishing Company, Inc. 2001.

Rudd, J. (Director). (2013). *American Blackout* [TV Movie]. National Geographic.

Sartorius, Matthias. (2014). *"Arctic: Future Bone of Contention?"* [Master's Thesis]. Global Studies Institute of the University of Geneva.

Slavo, Mac 2018. "Super EMP Capable of Disabling Power Grid Across Lower 48 States." *SHTFplan.com.* 20 June 2011. Retrieved from: www.shtfplan.com/emergency-preparedness/super-emp-capable-of-disabling-power-grid-across-lower-48-states_06202011

Schoen, Douglas E. with Evan Roth Smith. *Putin's Master Plan.* New York: Encounter Books, 2016.

"Senator Dan Sullivan (R-AK) Chairs an Arctic Military Readiness Hearing." *Youtube.* Uploaded by Senator Dan Sullivan, 4 March 2020, www.bing.com/videos/search?q=dan+sullivan+hearing+on+arctic+strategy&&view=detail&mid=9B0171BDCEFBAEE179A79B0171BDCEFBAEE179A7&&FORM=VRDGAR&ru=%2Fvideos%2Fsearch%3Fq%3Ddan%2Bsullivan%2Bhearing%2Bon%2Barctic%2Bstrategy%26FORM%3DHDRSC3

Sjordal, Carly. 2019. "Senator Murkowski introduces bill to build a Department of Defense Arctic Security Studies Center." *Webcenter11.com/KTVF,* 31

October 2019. Retrieved from www.webcenter11.com/content/news/Senator-Murkowski-introduces-bill-to-build-a-Department-of-Defense-Arctic-Security-Studies-Center-564199211.html

Spencer, Emily. *Solving the People Puzzle. Cultural Intelligence and Special Operations Forces.* Toronto: Dundurn Press. 2010.

State of Alaska Emergency Operations Plan 2016 (Updated 2018). Retrieved from: www.coursehero.com/file/42104789/2018-SOA-EOPpdf/
Summary of the 2018 National Defense Strategy. Retrieved from: dod.defense.gov/Portals/1/Documents/pubs/2018-National-Defense-Strategy-Summary.pdf

Taber, Robert. *War of the Flea: The Classic Study of Guerrilla Warfare.* Dulles, Virginia. Potomac Books. 2002.
Tadjdeh, Yasmin. 2015. "Russia Expands Military Presence in the Arctic." *National Defense,* Vol. 100 (745): pp. 34-35.

The Department of the Air Force Arctic Strategy. July 2020. Retrieved from: www.af.mil/Portals/1/documents/2020SAF/July/ArcticStrategy.pdf

The Department of the Army Arctic Strategy, *"Regaining Arctic Dominance,"* March 2021. Retrieved from: https://api.army.mil/e2/c/downloads/2021/03/15/9944046e/regaining-arctic-dominance-us-army-in-the-arctic-19-january-2021-unclassified.pdf

Thiessen, Mark. "Russian submarine surfaces near Alaska during war exercise." *The Associated Press*. 27 August 2020. Retrieved from: https://www.militarytimes.com/news/your-military/2020/08/27/russian-submarine-surfaces-near-alaska-during-war-exercise/

Törnberg, Peter. 2018. "Echo Chambers and Viral Misinformation: Modeling Fake News as Complex Contagion." *PLoS ONE* 13 (9): 1–21. doi:10.1371/journal.pone.0203958.

Tuunainen, Pasi. 2014. "New Approaches to the study of Arctic warfare." *Nordia Geographical Publications,* 43:1, 87-99. Retrieved from: https://www.researchgate.net/publication/275350339_New_approaches_to_the_study_of_Arctic_warfare

United States Senator for Alaska Lisa Murkowski. 2020. "Murkowski Stresses Need to Equip DoD with Tools to Support Arctic Defense Strategy, Promotes Ted Stevens Arctic Center for Security Studies." Press Release, 19 November 2019. Retrieved from: https://www.murkowski.senate.gov/press/release/murkowski-stresses-need-to-equip-dod-with-tools-to-support-arctic-defense-strategy-

University of Alaska Fairbanks. 2010. "Alaska Native Cultures and Issues: Responses to frequently asked questions." Edited by Libby Roderick. University of Alaska Press Fairbanks.

Wilson Center, July 2020. "The U.S. Air Force Arctic Strategy, Alaska, and the New Arctic: A Conversation with Alaska's Senators Lisa Murkowski and Dan Sullivan." Retrieved from: https://www.wilsoncenter.org/event/us-air-force-arctic-strategy-alaska-and-new-arctic-conversation-alaskas-senators-lisa

Wikipedia. *"Russian Airborne Forces."* Retrieved from: https://en.wikipedia.org/wiki/Russian_Airborne_Forces

Wikipedia. *"Winter War."* Retrieved from: https://en.wikipedia.org/wiki/Winter_War#Finnish_guerrilla_tactics

Wikipedia. *"3M-54 Kalibr Missile."* Retrieved from: https://en.wikipedia.org/wiki/3M-54_Kalibr

Woody, Christopher. 2021. "The US Army wants to regain 'dominance' in the Arctic, and it's looking all over the world for help." *Business Insider.* 27 April 2021. Retrieved from: https:// The US Army wants to regain 'dominance' in the Arctic, and it's looking all over the world for help (msn.com)

Yousaff, Mohammad & Adkin, Mark. "The Battle for Afghanistan: The Soviets Versus The Mujahideen During the 1980's." South Yorkshire: Pen & Sword Books, Ltd. 2007.

Youtube. 2016. "New York News Coverage of the Blackout of 2003." 4 May 2016. Retrieved from: https://www.bing.com/videos/riverview/relatedvideo?q=New+York+news+coverage+of+the+blackout+of+2003&mid=C995D